"I will give this book to my daughter to read. Zoe's insight into the way the world works is important to know/realize, and things that most people wouldn't think about on their own. She is a true role model."
Deborah Ruth Felsenfeld, A Scribe Transcripts, *listed in the San Francisco Reel Directory, as well as Southern Oregon Film & Television (SOFaT).*

"*FLIRTonomics* will open your heart and fill your purse with value. Use Zoe's strategies to discover how to fully express yourself without manipulation by tapping into all of your feminine assets and connecting for capital gains."
Sherrie Rose, Love Linguist and Liking Authority

"Zoe Sexton presents a creative, thought-provoking approach to human relationships, flirting and the power of personal capital in moving the forces of the world. Her unique perspective redefines FLIRT, giving it power and grace."
Brandon Wade, Founder and CEO of InfoSystems,
Bestselling Author of *Connecting with the "IN" Crowd*

"Ever wondered how some people seem to have the "IT" Factor, easily attracting business and personal success? In her new book *Flirtonomics*, Zoe Sexton reveals the secret recipe, the power of FLIRT, to creating an irresistible presence and influence."
Adryenn Ashley, CEO Wow! Is Me,
Business Architect/Startup Advisor and
Award Winning Best Selling Author of *Every Single Girl's Guide to Her Future Husband's Last Divorce*

"Simply put, charisma is the secret sauce in getting ahead in business. People are attracted to energetic, bright, confident people, and, thus, it's easier to do business with them. *FLIRTonomics* can help teach women social techniques to improve business interactions with other women and men without the fear it may send the wrong signals."
Alicia Dunams, International Speaker and author of
Goal Digger: Lessons Learned from the Rich Men I Dated

"In her ground-breaking book *Flirtonomics,* Zoe Sexton addresses how the cultivation of women's femininity and charisma can give them a professional as well as personal advantage in leadership positions. *Flirtonomics* is destined to change the way people think about personal assets and female leadership from page one."

Karen Solomon, Image Consultant, Author,
Speaker on the subjects of Sex, Money & Relationship
and the importance of communication. Co-author of *Savvy
Leadership Strategies for Women.*

In this book, Zoe has proven herself to be much more than just a pretty face, she is brilliant. It is evident Zoe has done the research and is bringing forth her findings to help empower men and women alike. She's got me thinking in a whole new way about how to build on my God-given assets with integrity to both help me be more successful in life, and help others achieve the same. This woman is all heart!

Ana Maria Sanchez, M.S. Empowerment Counselor
& Best Selling Author of *Girl From The Hood Gone Good*

FLIRTonomics

HOW TO CAPITALIZE ON YOUR FEMININITY AND
CHARISMA WITHOUT SLEEPING WITH ANYONE

ZOE SEXTON, MBA

Published by Bush Street Press
237 Kearny Street, #174
San Francisco, CA 94108
415-413-0785

Copyright© Zoe Sexton, 2012

ISBN Print 978-1-937445-30-0
ISBN e-Book 978-1-937445-31-7

Library of Congress Control Number 2012938214

Printed in the United States of America

DEDICATION

This book is dedicated to women everywhere and to the men who appreciate them. It is dedicated to the progress of women and the opening of a global conversation challenging restrictions and barriers that stand in its way. It is also with special dedication to my own daughters, Brooke Baldwin and Brianna McInnis, and my sons, Cody Baldwin and Chad McInnis, as well as my mother, Karen Sexton, who taught me to be sensitive and aware of the natural world and cause and effect.

ACKNOWLEDGEMENTS

There are so many people to give thanks to here; I could go on for pages. I am truly grateful for all of the friends and family who have supported my creative process and the ups and downs as I discovered how I wanted to say these words out loud. My gratitude list includes not only friends, friends, family and supporters, but also people who have affected me and helped me take direction and form decisions on this journey. There are no neutral moves any more than there are meaningless connections. Everything matters.

I will start with my publisher, Alicia Dunams, female entrepreneur powerhouse, who is a great friend and the driver to my completion of this book. Rie Langdon and Patti McKenna, editors and layout. Zoe Lonergan, cover design. Friends and family who have supported this process in so many ways: Karen Sexton (mother, teacher editor), Deva Sexton-Putney, Mike Sutton (friend, editor), Steve Manning, James McInnis, Travis Kelleher, Robert May, Mara Williams, Brandon Wade, Fred Larson (photography and discovery), and Lanae St. John for her wisdom and practicality. The women I interviewed, Mira Leda, Jessica Scorpio, Allana Pratt, who allowed me to see how they leverage their femininity and charisma personally and professionally, and many others not quoted specifically. Women like Adryenn Ashley, Jeanette Vonier and Michelle Van Otten who inspire and support their clients' growth and change to confidence and fame. A Band of Wives (ABOW) in Marin, my Facebook friends, and business connections: I learn from you every day. My training at Smith Barney, which provided the education I spun off into Financial

Fitness workshops and led me to the concept of Your 401k Plan for Life, the personal development program for men and women. Catherine Hakim for her book, *Erotic Capital*, that got me thinking about a more holistic approach and how it's the Social Handicap that is keeping women at an economic deficit. To those of you who taught me both the lessons of rejection and the lessons of energetic engagement where I watched you create and become inspired. Life's a journey, and more than that, an adventure.

TABLE OF CONTENTS

AN EXPLANATORY NOTE

This book is fundamentally about communication. It's about considering all the ways we communicate and the tools we use to do so. It is not about manipulation or trickery. FLIRTonomics is about using our personal assets and skills to communicate authentically, get the value we deserve, and have fun while doing it.

For women, these assets include our femininity, charisma, beauty, and our intelligence. While these assets are innate and natural, when used in business, competitors may misconstrue them as manipulation. As women, it's our right to develop and use these assets because they belong to us—they make us women and draw on the essence of who we are. To not use them is like buying the most fabulous dress and never wearing it to a party, or like asking a man to become a woman. It's not fair or reasonable.

The subtitle, *How to capitalize on our femininity and charisma without sleeping with anyone,* was chosen because women don't need to trade their assets for anyone's sexual pleasure. In fact, they have far more value when they do not.

To get started, let me define a few terms:

FLIRT—an acronym for Friendly, Leadership, Inquisitive, Receptive, Tactile.

Charisma –social grace, harnessed sexuality, mindfulness, and leadership.

Femininity—process oriented, interdependent, spiritually centered, and body type.

Flirtonomics—the economic use of FLIRT for capital gains.

Capital—products or goods that can be exchanged for one another.

Cultural Capital—education, vocation, beliefs and arts, or skills of value.

Social Capital—network or connections for professional or personal growth.

Economics—the creation, distribution, and consumption of goods and services.

Erotic—derivative of Eros, the god of love, which is to move, to stir, and put into motion.

Metta—Loving kindness.

These terms will appear throughout the context of this book. We are re-framing and re-constructing some key terms in cultural and social behavior to free them for your best use.

FLIRTonomics is about giving the gift of love and intention to anyone you choose and building relationships with ease and grace. FLIRTing as defined in the context of this book is the friendly gift of energetic engagement you can have with anyone of any age at any time. It's time for the attributes of the personality ethic and the value-driven attributes of the principle ethic to come together. Kindness, interdependence, and clarity of intention are essential in our human relationships. It's not business; it is personal. **FLIRT specifically refers to being Friendly, exhibiting Leadership, and being Inquisitive, Receptive, and Tactile in our relationships.**

As such, FLIRTonomics addresses our personal assets from the inside out and how we use them appearance, body language, verbal words, pace, and tones of voice are important and illustrate the context in which we find ourselves, as well as the authenticity in our engagement with others. What we signify by our dress, our posture, and our facial expression either opens or closes doors, personally and professionally. How we accept and extend eye contact, our hand, or a note tells more than the gesture. We are always communicating, biologically, mentally, physically, emotionally, intellectually, and spiritually. In this way, our intentions become evident. There are significant differences between men and women in the ways they communicate and their interpretation of social communication. These differences are filtered, as we design our own communications, develop our personal attributes, and use them to reach our goals.

There are no neutral moves in our bodies, our appearance, or in our intentions. When we FLIRT or add it into our communications, we bring fun, laughter, smiling, and biological responses into our contact with others. Our interactions are physiological and biological, as well as intellectual. The human brain and our internal biology (intuition) are always gathering information and translating it for us. If we can begin to notice what others are telling us before we engage verbally, and while we are doing so, we might build a more compassionate and enthusiastic society. We might even begin to experience joy on a daily basis.

Flirting is a form of positive energetic engagement. It demonstrates attraction in a positive, non-sexual way, and in the context of this book, any sexual component is secondary in nature. While FLIRTing *can* be an indicator of romantic interest between two people and can certainly be used to indicate attraction, the broader power of FLIRT is one that can change your economic and social status. FLIRT opens the doors to laughter and friendships by deepening interactions and creating positive memory experience associations.

For a period, I wrote for a dating site that addressed the issues of men, women, and economic capital. Economics and dating were two practical and related topics, which makes sense. It costs money to date, whether you are male or female, spending it on the dinner, a babysitter, gas, parking, cosmetics, clothing, and any number of items women "need" to make ourselves more attractive to the opposite sex. As the moderator of a dating site under a pseudonym, I helped members navigate communication blunders and misplaced expectations in their dating experiences and around money. It became so clear, so quickly, in the world of sex, dating, and money that a woman's presence, beauty, femininity, and social grace have economic value. They also have economic value in social and professional environments. For people in the dating process, leveraging their personal capital is a full-time job while searching for a mate. Outside of the romantic attraction process, women have been discouraged from using their personal assets to engage. Women have been strongly discouraged from using their attributes outside of the dating environment to get their jobs done more effectively. As such, the attributes of femininity and charisma in women become imbalanced through a woman's life and go untapped and unrecognized in many of their relationships.

As women in all environments and in many roles, including work and relationships, we are most successful when we can access and use our whole beings to perform our duties. Many of us have been living with a false sense of who we are—we are out of synch with our essence and what behaviors are socially acceptable because societal norms have made it difficult to find our place. Our inability to connect with others and take action from our deepest core has created a disparity among us and is a source of sickness, both personally and in our environment. Perhaps this is why there are so many support groups for women geared at reawakening their femininity and sexuality.

It's a contradiction to be labeled with negatives and social stigma while we enhance and develop our personal assets via the beauty industry for use only within a specific framework. Who wouldn't eventually implode if they were directed to use only a portion of their natural talents? Constrains of social behavior, unfriendly labels, and name-calling have held women back economically to the tune of $.80 for every $1.00 a man earns. Fear and competitive behaviors that go against the grain of who we are have kept women from expressing their femininity, humor, and unique ability to engage. The good news is we can wake up and improve not only our economic status, but also our sense of happiness and connectedness. We influence others positively by taking a few steps and strengthening certain aspects of ourselves. Developing FLIRT, your femininity, and charisma (harnessed sexuality combined with social grace and vital energy) will give you a professional and personal advantage by bringing out the joyous leader in you.

I was not an attractive child and was not popular in school. In fact, when I was a child, I was teased and harassed in a very unfriendly manner throughout grade school. Despite doing well in school, I became so introverted I could not talk to kids my own age comfortably. I was not invited to school parties or other social events because everything I did, from facial expression to body language, communicated I did not want to be invited. I was terrified and felt different. I never considered my physical attractiveness until I was in my 30's, but focused my energy on other aspects of personal development, learning, my personal beliefs, attitudes, behaviors, and communications with others.

Anyone can become more attractive through their health, behaviors, and intentions. Throughout my life, I have made very powerful connections with people that led to deep, long-term friendships rather than romantic relationships. The fact is any woman can find a romantic encounter—the trick is to convert misplaced romantic interest to pure energy and channel it into amazing partnerships, friendships, and business opportunities where all parties win. Misplaced romantic interest is simply energy. Energy is powerful, *and* it is transferrable. Passion can be directed for other creative purposes, whether in business or in social change. This is the highest level of transformation using FLIRT.

FLIRTONOMICS

My life is an adventure, filled with unique experiences supporting my value system. The adventures always began with a little FLIRT, some charisma, and an open attitude. I found myself a guest of the Korean delegation at the World Energy Congress in Montreal; being driven all over the SFO tamarack in a beverage truck at high speeds, getting on the plane late, and telling the pilot I was the daughter of a visiting ambassador to San Francisco, after going through all sorts of high-level security; at the age of 12, negotiating the purchase of a race horse from ranchers who had taken her over for non-payment of pasture; traveling to Las Vegas to sit on the panel of a multi-million dollar software company; on the Board of Directors of a breast cancer foundation and one for Lyme disease; hitchhiking through Australia and serving the Australian Wine Society at their annual dinner; helping a socialite on her writing project; training horses for endurance racing in Southern California; and building a 3,000 square foot custom home in five and a half months, while directing 40 subcontractors on the jobsite.

My adventures are too many to list here, and they involve women, men, children, young and old, thick or thin. Opening up to and accessing all of your personal capital will allow you to connect with people more deeply. It allows you to be more effective and powerful in your work and your passions. When you bring a sense of adventure into life, others want to be involved, creating the juiciest moments in life. Being visible helps tremendously, and it builds a personal brand. Charisma, femininity, and humor make things happen—let them make things happen for you now!

CHAPTER 1

What is FLIRTonomics?

The best way to predict the future is to create it.
~ Peter Drucker

FLIRTonomics is the ability to create gain (environmental, situational, economic, social, or cultural) by using certain aspects of engagement to connect with others. FLIRTonomics uses active engagement and fun to facilitate relationships that build business and social change. FLIRT paves the way to get what you need in an effective and efficient way. It's about balance and abundance. FLIRT helps women access and develop all of their personal capital and exchange it for other forms of capital.

Flirting in the traditional sense is defined by the following attributes:

- Speaking and behaving in a way slightly more familiar and intimate than the relationship between the parties would indicate, *within the rules of social etiquette.*
- Using body language
- Using tone of voice
- Culture and context

Economics is the creation, distribution, and consumption of goods or services. When something is economical, it creates residual or savings. FLIRT and FLIRTing can be seen in the same context as a level of engagement creating lasting positive feelings. The residual energy and good will can be repurposed. The goods and services we are creating are positive interactions. The excess energy and positive feelings, just as in any other economic exchange, create profits and are available for investment. How we choose to save or invest the excess is up to us. Once we uncover how to get the highest profit from positive interactions, the possibilities are endless. In fact, this is just the catalyst as it gets things moving quickly.

WHY USE FLIRT

What is holding you back from your full potential? FLIRTonomics dictates you CAN use your femininity and charisma to acquire or move capital and gather support for your causes.

Uses of FLIRTonomics	Example
Shift economic capital for personal wealth	Sell your personal goods and services using FLIRT as your sales tool.
Build long-term relationships	Follow up with people you meet, bond with people who have the same interests. Connect through experiences.
Increase inner vitality and longevity	Breathe deep, smile, and get some exercise by walking through a public place.
Connect and engage with others	Say hello and drop your guard; it produces dopamine in your system-making you feel good.
Make friends	Be friendly and then take numbers when people indicate further connection interests. Say yes.
Build social capital	Use your social skills as an asset to increase value for friends and causes.

Build cultural capital	Get a deal on a class or training program and attend with a friend.
Build economic equality	Use your charm to make things easier at work instead of more difficult. Ask how you can help.
Get a new job	Practice your social grace and poise, then ask for the money. Negotiate.
Get a pay raise	Ask for a raise with feminine focus; don't move until you get it.
Fulfill goals	Share your goals with a friend and reach them together.
Get financing for a company	Put together a dream team and use your skills to open doors and make friendly business.
Become a leader	Build your charisma and power of attraction.
Develop self-esteem	By making new friends and socializing with them or accomplishing goals.
Increase total personal wealth and value	Use FLIRT to create strong partnerships and reach agreements.
Philanthropy	Use your FLIRT to build relationships that support causes and create change.

I created the acronym for FLIRT to dispel any preconceived negative stigmas and reframe FLIRTing in your mind. Consider the concept of being:

FLIRT:

Friendly, Leadership, Inquisitive, Receptive, Tactile

Friendly

Do you have enough vitality to feel friendly? Do you feel you have the energy you need to accomplish all the tasks you have throughout the day, with energy to spare? Liveliness is an outer expression of your inner vitality and health. It is expressed in happiness, laughter, emotion, enthusiasm, curiosity, and supportive joy. It shows you are getting enough vitamins and oxygen into your bloodstream, so your body and mind are functioning in tandem.

Being friendly may seem like a strange thing to suggest, but I was surprised by people who said they did not want to be "friendly." They thought it was "too much work." This reminds me of people who say they do not want to be wealthy because they don't want to work that hard. In the meantime, they are too busy for coffee or a phone call because they are literally running themselves ragged. You think those other folks who are taking a walk, going on vacation, or spending time with friends and family are working harder than you? It is highly unlikely.

When you are in balance physically and emotionally, you have excess energy to share. You will feel more inclined to be friendly when you feel positive about yourself. Strangely, it works both ways. By behaving in a friendly or helpful manner, the energy and balance manifest inside you.

At the same time, being friendly increases your presence in your community and the positive value you place in yourself. It takes very little energy—sometimes just a shift in posture, attitude, and facial expression. Being friendly to others is an act of kindness to others or yourself. A lack of desire to be friendly demonstrates a sense of disconnectedness. There may be nothing wrong with it as long as your happiness quotient is measuring up to your own standards and desires. Just remember, while it is something you GIVE to others and is generous, it is also something you receive.

Leadership

This is a key aspect of what you become when you use your charisma assertively and take steps to set yourself apart. In 1996, William Drucker wrote about leaders of the future in his book of the same name. At the very end, he puts out some interesting warnings to women and "people of color," as he describes them. Not only can he see these two groups as leaders in the future, and they are, as his book was published in 1996, but he warns us to beware of stereotypes and old assumptions that can hold us back, as well as make an assault on our roles. Leaders must stay true to their values and watch for the double standard where men are lauded for their enthusiasm and passion, while women are labeled as emotional or hysterical, Drucker says. He saw in advance the terrain ahead and the skills needed for the roles.

Leaders are cultural architects. Women are natural architects and influencers of culture, often behind the scenes. As a leader you communicate, articulate, and negotiate the change you desire while you impassion your supporters. Your perseverance, humor, and integrity are leadership traits. William Drucker states that, "Intuition and non-verbal communication skills will be critical to leadership." Pp 312, *Leader of the Future*. Women are known for being intuitive, so it seems only natural to fully develop that and all of your assets to use in leadership.

Inquisitive

Being inquisitive means taking an interest in people and their situations. Asking questions is integral to developing your charisma. Curiosity can lead to adventure because it leads to discovery. People who are curious tend to have a more diverse way of seeing the world and finding solutions to problems. Your curiosity about others, their experiences, their feelings, and their interactions creates connection and makes life interesting. An interesting life is worth living. Seeing the details and finding gratitude breeds curiosity and expands our perception of the world. It becomes multidimensional.

Yet kids are often discouraged from being too curious. "Curiosity killed the cat" used to be the saying, though I have rarely heard it used in recent years. This attitude was more commonly applied to girls than to young boys. It was a standard assumption that young men would seek adventure, but young women would not. Only our heroines were curious and broke all the rules. Taking in the experiences of others broadens and opens our minds to new ideas and new relationships.

Receptive

Receive the information you are being given throughout the day. Sometimes it is intuitive information. Sometimes it comes to you in a dream. Sometimes it is right in front of you as if you are watching things collide in slow motion. Being receptive means listening, paying attention, and being objective. When you are objective, you do not pass judgment—you gain perspective on a topic or situation and try to see sides other than your own. Our personal perception is limiting. It can slowly build a silent wall around us in such a way we may not even notice it is being built. It can be deceptive and insidious if we do not make a practice of listening to the viewpoints of others. Understanding that all information must pass through the filters of all our own self-constructed stories *(which may or may not be true)* lends some perspective on the matter. Being receptive allows you to find and enjoy new experiences and opportunities. You may find out you do like something or someone more than you thought when you open up to see things in more ways than one.

Tactile

Tactile is about the sensation of touch, comfort, nurture, touching, or wanting to be touched. Humans are tactile creatures, yet many of us find ourselves starved for touch or contact. A touch can soothe nerves, heal cuts and bruises, and connect for life. A mother hugs her child, friends hug each other, we shake hands, and kiss cheeks, yet many people in our society are starved for touch. We have a fear of germs or liabilities in other forms that keep us separated. Plastics and films are used to nullify our touch, and we must pay to be touched through massage and physical therapies, if we can afford it.

With such pressure and stigmas being enforced around touch, it is not surprising people have forgotten the nuances between appropriate and inappropriate touch. I strongly encourage touching to connect. This is generally done in an accepted greeting of the hand, arm, shoulder, cheek, or a hug. It is usually not acceptable to touch people on the chest or lower body parts, or for extended periods of time. An example of inappropriate touch or misguided touch is the handshake where some people feel they can extend the length of a hug, touch, or eye contact. The handshake that overpowers or is painful is also poor and shameful behavior. This is not okay and demonstrates lack of respect for the other person since it is self serving. Do not do things that make other people uncomfortable. Try to notice if you do and correct immediately.

FLIRT IS ECONOMICAL

When we say something is economical, we mean it saves money, time, or something else of value. For example, when you buy something "on sale," you have created a savings and can spend that savings on something else of your choosing. FLIRTing is economical. It can save time, money, face, energy, and embarrassment. It can get things moving more efficiently, effectively, and enjoyably. Flirting saves time when it enables you to do something faster—for example, getting service at the bank or streamlining processes for the purchase of a product. Upbeat engagement can make a tedious phone call go faster and easier. A phone sales representative may do a little extra for the person who is pleasant, engaging, and open during the conversation versus the person who is irritated and brittle.

When most people think of economics, they think of the money or economic capital used to purchase goods and services. While FLIRT is not directly used in exchange for money, it can allow you to make more money, acquire more money, build your own social network, or cause the movement of money from one place to another. FLIRTonomics addresses the use of flirting, social charm, and charisma to create momentum in the economic flow. It also addresses the concept of total health maintenance because our optimal health is a product of inner and outer attendance, as well as our mental and emotional states.

Economics is a social science that studies the behavior of consumers and suppliers. It is the development, distribution, and consumption of products, goods, or services (in whatever form they come). In the world of economics, the idea is to create excess because the extra value continues the momentum and creates profits. In a simple example, if beans are produced for $1 dollar per pound and sold for $2 per pound, the profit is $1 dollar. This excess is absorbed and reinvested in production, the capital markets, households, or other investible assets. It continues its momentum into the economy, either to expand growth of the farm, the household, or in this case, something else. It can be saved, but it never really stops moving. If there is no excess profit, it is hard for the farmer to do more than produce beans. She won't be able to support her family, send her kids to school, or buy other types of food. This process is economic flow. FLIRT produces energy and activates brain response, converting it into economic flow.

The benefits of FLIRT should be obvious, but why are they so overlooked and even frowned upon? Should we so easily forget to make our femininity and charisma a part of who we are?

Over the years, I have spoken with many women about jobs and family. Some women, who are now over 48 years old, worked very hard and in stiff competition with men in their quest for equal economic pay. They were often single and sometimes childless, whether they wanted to be or not. They made a choice to be competitive, and, as a result, ran out of time to build families. They did not use the foundation of FLIRT to open doors and build relationships because they did not want social stigma, labeling, or just felt it was "wrong." They preferred to operate within the context of male assessments and judgments with a *social handicap* when it came to overall outcome and performance. They resented the inequality and often did not know why because their innate skills had been socialized out of them. They let the tools that could give them a leg up languish on the sidelines. Or perhaps the constant role-play of wearing the masculine form in the work environment was exhausting—always an actress, never the transformation.

Then I interviewed entrepreneurial women of the younger generation, from 23 to 45 years old. I was pleasantly surprised by their progressive attitudes toward femininity, charisma, and using FLIRT to create better relationships at work and at home. These women are making strides toward equal economic pay, as well as fully embracing their femininity and personal asset portfolio.

Disapproval of women using their feminine charisma to create change starts young and is then solidified by labeling and name calling. It was created long ago as part of a patriarchal society that we have adapted to in many ways. As women, we not only accept this, but we often support it as we frown and fret upon our own daughters and their developing sensuality. There are useful standards of behavior. The primary guidelines are compassion, kindness, and mindfulness. With these in hand, most of the other rules and regulations fall away as they are no longer needed. It's an old value system and language used to define roles that supported a society with different needs than those we have today. FLIRT is the new language for a more transparent value system in a progressive society.

FLIRT knows no gender or age. It was flirting that led to one of my longest and dearest friendships when a two-year-old boy engaged with me in line at a coffee shop. He was sitting in the low stroller, smiling and trying to attract my attention while I was in line, so I started talking with him. His mom was a tall, attractive, and very pregnant blonde. She was rather surprised and not so thrilled about talking with a non-pregnant mom, but after I was talking with her son a bit, she began to engage with me, as well. Finally, as we carried our conversation outside, she pulled out a card and mumbled that she NEVER did this, but would love it if I called her. Much to my own surprise, I did, and began a wonderful decades-long friendship between her husband, kids, and my family. We have remained friends over 16 years; I wrote her son's Bar Mitzvah brochure, and she is the godmother of my youngest daughter. Just say yes and follow up. You never know who you will meet.

SOCIAL HANDICAP

Our societal constraints encourage women to operate at a fraction of their power and capacity. They are essentially discouraged from using their "feminine ways" to make things happen and get what they want. I have yet to hear men being discouraged from using their masculine ways; in fact, they are encouraged to use their innate assets. I call this the Social Handicap, and women have been playing with it for a long time. When you operate at a fraction of your ability, it is considered to be a disadvantage. If you are not using your skills at full capacity in a competitive environment, you are less likely to be as successful. Sometimes these skills are hidden, sometimes they are physical or mental, and at other times, they are socially imposed. When women have skills and are discouraged from, or even ostracized for, using them, it should be considered a societal waste. In the past 20 years, there have been thousands of personal development books, programs, meditations, efforts, affirmations, and therapists dedicated to the idea of awakening and changing behaviors and beliefs that have been accepted or imposed on women. Yet, they do not expose or encourage women to use the assets of their gender or birthright. Now we are doing just that.

Women should be able to use whatever tools they need to achieve the goals they want. Men use whatever tools necessary to rise to the top, so women shouldn't be afraid to do what they need to do while still acting in a dignified and honorable way. ~Mira Veda, Founder LipstickandPolitics.com

In etymology, handicap means to put at a disadvantage. It indicates the weaker party was given an advantage in the outcome over a more experienced player. Handicaps, often used in the context of horse racing, golf, or board games like chess, are occasions where the superior player is given a disability. This can be seen as a universal condition, but also as an opportunity to create change. The use of femininity and charisma for women means shedding the Social Handicaps placed on many of us at a young age and taking a position of economic and social equality.

This is not the same as men being discouraged from crying. Neither gender is encouraged to cry because it demonstrates a discomfort that makes the group uncomfortable as a whole. It indicates pain and lack of health in the instant it occurs, so people react and tune into it as they should. Cries are our earliest form of communication, and the type of crying tells everything about the action needed to make it stop. There are very biological reasons for this, and regardless of gender, people must cry as a form of communication. A more effective example might be men feigning toughness. This is fear-based, unauthentic behavior. Our society is trying to get rid of the need for it through studies of the brain, awareness development, and neutralizing the need for aggression.

As women have become more liberated, they have shed some of the weight of the handicap, but these social views are supported by genders, as well as religious institutions and cultural law. Social role assignment intrinsically implements handicaps and allowances in behavior. Social behavior is defined by the culture it exists in as a framework for communication and station. Pushing the envelope in interaction is worth an extension when it's done with awareness and respect.

In horse racing, the handicap is based on pace, form, class, post position, jockey, and variable factors specific to the event. How is this applied to women? Socially, we measure and implement our own personal handicaps on people we do business with or meet. We take into account someone's attractiveness, integrity, and situation as we consider our involvement. These measurements are personal to our own experiences and judgments. Eventually, people reveal themselves, but a little FLIRT can go a long way in demonstrating our ability to work well with others and create ease in the work environment. Handicaps in horse racing are implemented based on the "body language" of the horse and past records. Handicaps on women are distributed based on appearance, body language, and socially and culturally accepted behaviors. The reasons behind them and their necessity are what is being challenged here.

"Nobody accuses David Beckham of selling out or being a less competitive athlete because he poses in underwear. But when female Olympic athletes use their sex appeal, they are condemned as anti-feminist." [by other women] *Brian Alexander, http://bodyodd.msnbc.msn.com/_news/2011/09/23*

Women who use the power of their charisma and femininity in the workplace achieve higher paying positions sooner. Catherine Hakim, author of the book *Erotic Capital*, wrote that beauty and self-presentation equate to a 10 to 20% higher premium in pay than people who do not use it. When you consider the fact that women continue to earn $.82 to the $1.00 earned by a man in their same field, it looks like a path toward economic equality. She also mentions that Western culture rewards it less than other cultures and discourages its use more when it is not in accepted venue and form (strip clubs and pornography).

Christine Legarde reflects Hakim's ideal for a modern woman with erotic capital. She exemplifies the smart, stylish, well-educated, charismatic leader who does not exude sexuality in her interactions. Her social skills, quick wit, and manners have leveraged her to the top position in the IMF. She is feminine, charismatic, highly intelligent, and competent. The sooner women discover, develop, and use their assets appropriately in the workplace, the faster they can reach economic equality.

Women who expressed happiness or contentment with their work and personal lives also openly discussed using their "womanly ways" and ability to engage as part of their process of getting movement or momentum in their companies.

"By the age of 30, I had a three-quarter-of-a-million-pound house, a Mercedes convertible (and a Mercedes estate for when I took my dogs out), a walk-in dressing room crammed with clothes that Carrie Bradshaw would be envious of — oh, and I had a generous six-figure salary and a high-ranking position in my chosen industry," says Samantha Brick, *about her use of feminine charisma to get ahead in a male-dominated industry. 8/25/2011 From: http://www.dailymail.co.uk.*

I propose this, in part, because women are competing for jobs with men and the terms of engagement have been predisposed by men. In order to compete in a male-dominated workforce, women are acting, dressing, and behaving like men. Of course, this can never work as well as being a woman, using all of her feminine charisma and skills to get the job done. Gender equality in economic fair pay can be accomplished by women operating at full capacity and being compensated for ALL of the work they do.

Acting masculine means taking on hormone-driven male traits versus human traits shared by men and women. Many women who reach the top level of pay and job titles have opted for that versus having a family or children. The woman with an economically successful career rarely has time to have children, get married, or feed outside interests altogether. It's true that there is a sprinkling of them, like Carly Fiorina, Barbara Boxer, Hillary Clinton, or Justice Ruth Bader Ginsburg, but they all have something in common: **Strategic use of their femininity, charisma, personal assets, and**

charm to secure top notch jobs, as well as high-level partners with whom they can combine efforts. There is nothing wrong with this choice. Leveraging charisma, creating partnerships, and getting higher pay to support these efforts makes sense in a world where caregivers (usually women) are not paid for that aspect of their job. Child rearing causes serious career breaks in American and other cultures. Having children and taking time off can set the provider of care (usually women) back on their career paths for years and even decades. This makes one or the other economically undesirable.

Since many women start their careers on a 20% lower pay scale than men, is it possible that if they leveraged all their assets to start higher in the economic scale, it would level the playing field over time? It's possible they could benefit more economically earlier in their careers, enabling them to take the time they need for family later. A woman's reproductive fertility is a transient thing. We are biologically different by design, yet social demands have caused economic inequalities for so many single parents today.

Eve Ensler, author of *The Vagina Monologues* and *I Am an Emotional Creature,* said societies take away the sexuality and joy of being a woman early, starting when we are children. We start removing it by frowning upon it early in life. The flirting, engagement, laughter, and communication we need as human beings connected in society starts a removal process at a young age. By the time we're teenagers, we're sexually confused or disoriented, and we don't really know how to relate. We sink further into this in our 20's as we enter the workforce, then we create families, and by the age of 40, we've gone totally flat. Now we need some Prozac, right?

THE SOLUTION

Begin to think of yourself as an asset and an investment. Consider your personal assets in different parts so they can be enhanced, developed, and cultured to maturity. Consider each asset to be part of the diversified portfolio that is you. Leverage these personal assets to gain more cultural, social, and economic capital so you can accomplish your goals in life. Do so using femininity and charisma.

CHAPTER 2

Your Personal Capital

No one can make you feel inferior without your consent.
~ Eleanor Roosevelt

Your personal capital is defined by everything you personally bring to the table for social, professional, and personal interactions. It is your charisma, femininity, beauty, self-presentation, social grace, creativity, intimacy skills, vitality, nurture, physical attributes, intelligence, and humor, along with your intentions. Each of these aspects of yourself adds value to the experience you create with others. Every aspect matters because they affect the fluidity, ease, and motivation of those you come into contact with, and they are balanced.

The prospect of developing your femininity, charisma, and personal assets is your 401k plan for life. Using your femininity to initiate change and create connections between people is one of your untapped resources that can shift the imbalance in economic power and create a better environment for our future. Femininity is beauty, sensuality, engagement, power, and your ability to nurture. Charisma is a combination of attributes, most easily recognized as leadership, but containing sexuality, charm, presentation, and intelligence. Although charisma is usually applied to men, it can be developed in anyone.

PERSONAL ASSETS

Beauty

Your facial beauty, skin, eyes, hair, teeth, and overall health can be seen right here, and that is beautiful.

Fitness

Your physical body, its weight, and how it moves.

Social Grace

The knowledge, behaviors, and mannerisms you have that allow you to move comfortably in social circles and make others comfortable with you.

Vitality

The energy and sense of health you share with others when you are with them.

Self-Presentation

How you present yourself and how skilled you are at looking the best for the situation at hand.

Intimacy Skills

Your talent in personal relationships is based on communications, action, and adventure. These skills are useful personally or professionally, easing transitions between the two.

Fertility/Creativity

Fertility of the body is valuable if you can bear children, and even more essentially of the mind, whether you can or cannot.

Nurture

The ability to nurture through care, comforting, and cooking is certainly an element of personal capital since it has capital value, but it is also a form of expression and communication.

Mindfulness
The attention you focus on anyone you are involved with.

Openness
The language you convey with your body and energy that allows others to share and express themselves with you.

Humor
A true sign of a healthy human is illustrated by their sense of humor, wit, and sense of joy.

Your Femininity
Femininity is the largest untapped resource in the world. It has been operating at half speed. If you learn to embrace your feminine power and shed the shroud of competitive Darwinian tea that so many have been sipping, you will be so far ahead of the game.

FEMININITY

Feminine traits are made up of socially and biologically defined factors. To the public, your femininity is displayed by your female shape and a set of behaviors, attributes, or traits associated with the female gender. These traits are admired by "society" as womanly, so they are based on a value system along with body language and shape that indicates the female form. The wonderful thing about femininity is that it is flexible and can exhibit soft, warm qualities and then demand strength and determination. Femininity is mysterious, beautiful, attractive, and alluring. It teases and entices with a subtle power that is unshakeable. In romance, it is thrilling. In business, it is tempered and must be done with the patience and firm skill of a negotiator.

Women make amazing partners, most often, the partners of men. In balance, these partnerships are the most powerful the world has seen. There is a reason behind the saying, "Behind every great man there is a great woman." It should be said, **"Beside** every great man there is a great woman." This is a matter of history in almost every occasion. There is much to be said for that. In no way am I suggesting one needs the other, but women are expert collaborators, delegators, and multi-taskers, which demands the ability to commandeer support systems. Women bring the skill of partnership and collaboration to the table. Femininity embodies the highest quality of interdependence.

Some famous women who embody the feminine ideal are Hilary Rodham Clinton of the USA, Ellen Johnson Sirleaf of Liberia, and Laura Chincilla of Costa Rica. They represent a "social" feminine ideal and leveraged their charisma to gain powerful voices across their nations. The first and foremost aspect of femininity is exhibiting that women care. Caring and self-awareness are key indicators of femininity. Women demonstrate this in their appearance, from their bodies to style and make-up, and through activities that involve others caring for them, from hair styles to massages and pedicures. A married woman's self-presentation can indicate the comfort and success of her partner. When women are cared for and "feel" attended to by themselves or others, they exude beauty, peace, and happiness.

The feminine is a completely different animal than the masculine. Masculine and feminine can work exceptionally well together, but they encounter serious turmoil when pitted against each other. As partners, they should be equal, but somehow society has designed the concept of competition around winning and losing. Women can leverage their feminine charisma and power to not only bring forth economic equality, but also show how it can work with all parties winning. That is an exchange of value for value.

SOME TYPICAL MALE VS. FEMALE PRINCIPLES OF BEHAVIOR

Competitive	Community
Independent	Interdependent
Autonomy	Connection
Judgment	Trust
Linear	Flow
Fixed	Transition
Removed	Receptive

Start to develop your femininity with attention to your external appearance and your inner attitude. Take time to get your wardrobe in order and learn to apply cosmetics if you use them. Find colors, tones, and cuts of clothing that are flattering to your feminine form. Dress the way you deserve to see yourself. Dress and present yourself as if you were someone you would like to meet. Remember what is cute and be a little zany. Move your body and explore the areas that are being held in, tight, or stiff.

EXERCISE

Consider how other people respond to you. Note if it is positive or negative. Try another approach by putting yourself together with more attention. Many people practice their smiles, walk, and voice in front of the mirror.

Notes on your experiments

1. _____
2. _____
3. _____
4. _____
5. _____
6. _____
7. _____
8. _____

PHOTO RELEASE

Looking at photographs and videos has been very effective for me. It was disturbing and very uncomfortable at first, though. I was helping several photographers with their business. After a couple of sessions, it was clear they had also helped me with my self-perception. I called it PhotoTherapy, but now Visual Release, in helping others experience the same effects. Unlike typical phototherapy techniques, we do not use or sport through still photographs. We do a photo shoot as the first step in personal re-branding from the inside out. How we operate is closely tied to our self-perception and the perception of the public. In this process, we offer a before and after photo shoot over a period of time, as well as video analysis for body language and self-presentation. The experience and the results have changed lives and been the leg up people needed before taking the reins themselves.

CASE STUDY

PhotoTherapy or Visual Release

A woman in her early 40's goes from emotionally devastated and talking about getting a facelift to modeling for two of the top agencies in the Bay Area.

The young woman approached Zoe and began to talk about her divorce, her two children, and the dilemmas she faced in leaving a long-term relationship. Her self-doubt and sense of failure had turned inward, and she began to talk about all types of quick-fix beauty remedies, as well as getting a facelift. Her self-scrutiny was so intense all she could focus on were the small lines that had become magnified to her every time she looked in the mirror. She was tortured by a sense of unworthiness.

Zoe saw an immediate solution based on her own experience and what she had witnessed when photographs had been taken of her. She devised a plan to get the young woman a private photo shoot with her Pulitzer-nominated photographer who was building his portraiture folio. She set the time to attend the photo shoot with the woman to make it comfortable, as well as provide direction.

The objective was to show the woman the essence of who she was and how others saw her in the best moments. These images would be the ones she would keep and use to reposition herself to herself and to the world. They would build confidence and leave a lasting legacy.

Private Coaching

One part of Zoe's private coaching and facilitation program includes intensive training that draw out her client's unique networking and business development skills. Zoe starts where her clients need to start, whether it is in their own self-talk or in the conversation they are having with the external world.

In Zoe's work, there are no neutral moves. Everything people do, from their intention to their presence, is communicating something to their counterparts.

The young woman arrived with several outfits, from sexy to serious. She reported that, "Just the experience of getting in front of the camera and seeing the images through the viewer played back to me was an awakening." She said she was able to see that the person she saw in the mirror was a result of her own emotional state, and the images gave her confirmation she could choose to think differently. She felt her mindset shift and saw the energy she could bring into an engagement as invaluable.

This new mindset, combined with some connections to people who could facilitate the process of getting into an agency, put the young woman's photos at Stars in less than three weeks. This helped the young woman establish new relationships, begin to earn money, and gain self-confidence.

This led the young woman to have some breathing room and take a different approach to her personal assets, as well as what she could bring to the table. She no longer felt solely dependent on the divorce situation.

Today, the young woman is getting called for multiple modeling jobs and acting as a mediator and mentor to other women going through the emotional trials of divorce. She has been asked to assist in many legal cases because her self-confidence is high and she has a sense of social grace and awareness of how painful a self-inflicted mindset can be.

"I have achieved more than I could have thought and had no idea of how things would have panned out. I put myself in the hands of Zoe and her photographer, and that was just the stepping off point for where I took myself."

In conclusion, Zoe's client achieved:
- A mindset shift which now makes self-awareness and positive thinking a natural behavior for her and those she mentors.
- Greater business development awareness for her, as well as an awareness of opportunity when it knocks.
- The young woman achieved over a 1,000% return on investment in bottom-line dollars!

YOUR CHARISMA

Charisma is combined attitude and right behaviors for emotional response. It is a quality of leadership and creates followers by its very nature. Some people insist that you either have it or you don't, but that is a cop-out. We can learn anything—the more we develop our inner vitality and our vibrational energy, the more charismatic we will be. Charisma is generally applied to men. It has a richer, deeper, meaningful connotation than the feminine version, "Social Grace." Charisma stands on its own, whereas social grace has the word *social* in front of it, implying its constriction to social guidelines.

Social grace is one aspect alone. Charisma is a combination of aspects. Charisma is sexuality, fitness, social grace, vitality, presentation, and fertility, often resulting in leadership or power roles. This leaves the term "social grace" a little hollow and lacking, so I want you to develop your charisma.

Charismatic people are not necessarily beautiful or handsome, yet they are compelling and magnetic, often sexy, and can create strong impulses of attraction. Some of this is related to their controlled, but present, sexuality, their charm and social skills, their self-presentation, and their apparent intention. They also tend to be mindful and attentive, which can come off as attraction. Some people can contrive their charisma without being kind or well intended, but this book is

43

not for them, and I will give you some clues on how to spot them.

Principal elements of charismatic people:

- Attractive/compelling/sexy
- Charming
- Physically fit, but not always
- Attentive
- Kind
- Mindful
- Well presented
- Humorous

Charisma is a leadership quality that builds teams through inspiration, passion, and energy, creating a common sense of purpose. Charismatic behavior is an art, so it must be learned as one would learn an art. There is first the study of the masters, and then there is the development of your own unique style and vision. Fake behaviors and intentions are easy to spot. Do not make this mistake with misguided intentions. Charismatic people do not imitate each other. Their unique style and message are what makes them leaders and charismatic.

Charisma is developed through learned behaviors, which start with principles, then become habits.

Ten steps to learning charisma:

1. Smile with sincerity
2. Make eye contact
3. Be interested
4. Have a solid and warm handshake
5. Use mirroring
6. Pace the conversation and listen
7. Remember names and situations
8. Appear confident and relaxed

9. Harness your energy

10. Offer to help

For example, approach someone at an event by first going through the non-verbal process of connecting. Stand near them, make eye contact, and smile, opening the floor for verbal interaction. Find out about the person by being inquisitive. Listen and be receptive to their response. Mirror their body language back to them so they know you are listening to them with all that you have to offer. Be relaxed so they can relax. Offer to share some information, a contact, or an interest with them based on what they have expressed they are looking for.

Smiling is the universal language. It shows that we are friendly, harmless (we can usually detect the wicked smile), and approachable. Smiling opens doors and makes our passage from one venue to another safe and easier. Smiling draws people to you and creates instant joy. Making sincere eye contact without being inappropriate is important. Good solid eye contact tells people a lot about you through what they see in your eyes. Your eyes demonstrate your health and often your intentions. Eyes can be warm, cold, friendly, or unfriendly. Biologically, the eyes are moving all of the time. When we look at people, we sense their movements, even if their meaning is not literally translated back into our brain language. They provide clues to our neurology and our internal desires. Small movements in our eyes can depict a difference between what we are looking at and what we are thinking. Charismatic people move all their focus to the person they are engaged with, their eyes, their thoughts, and their intentions. People who do not learn eye-intention focus will have less success connecting and may appear inattentive or insincere.

Be interested in the person you are engaged with. Give them your energy. Ask questions and remember the answers. Interested people are interesting to others. Your body language, eye contact, and conversation indicate interest. If you sit down and cross your arms, it shows you are closed off to the other person. Maintain open body language and your interest will be open, as well. Our thoughts follow our bodies, as our bodies follow our thoughts. Keeping our bodies in the position of open conversation enables that conversation to occur.

Your handshake should be warm, comforting, and solid. Many people fail the handshake test. The hands come toward each other, open, thumbs up. The purpose is to interlock the thumbs and place palms together. The purpose is not to inflict pain or impose power or control on the other person. It is meant to be genuine, show openness, and harmlessness. It shows that we are open to agreement and making agreements. Some people never learn this, or they try to prove their strength against the other person. This is insincere and uncharismatic. It also breeds distrust.

Use mirroring to communicate with your counterpart. Learn their body language and mirror techniques and use them to communicate back to them. Mirroring is an innate behavior and can be used to bring people into agreement and trust. Its base is biological.

Take acting, toast masters, voice lessons, and get phototherapy and video analysis. Come to understand what it is you communicate to people and how you communicate it; then learn to do it better. Do not be afraid to really speak your mind—just remember, charismatic leaders do so with respect and an in-depth understanding of who their audience is. Talk about subjects, people, and experiences, other than your own. Being offensive is not charismatic. Notice quickly if you are offending people or when people become disinterested in what you have to say. Success demands more than being charismatic, so you had best be good at what you do and work continuously to get better at it. Leaders lead by example. Keep your dark side at bay unless you can access it with clever humor. People want to be around people who create energy, not suck it away.

- Dress to impress
- Do not gossip or offer back-talk
- Meet new people wherever you can
- Be honest, but not too frank or familiar – read your audience
- Help others in any way you can—try to do 10 deeds a day
- Respect the time of others by being punctual
- Stand up for yourself and your values
- Update your world knowledge and perspective so you can carry on any conversation
- Express gratitude
- Address and apologize for your mistakes
- Understand what you look like
- Do not be arrogant, keep right-sized
- Laugh a lot at yourself and situations

FORMS OF CAPITAL AND HOW THEY WORK

Economic capital refers to financial markets and generally to stocks, bonds, currencies, and commodities in any combination.

Social Capital refers to cooperation and confidence resulting in collective or economic gain. In sociology, it boils down to getting preferred treatment based on your social connections, but most importantly, how these human relations affect productivity and groups. The term social capital first appeared in a 1916 article by LJ Hanifan in reference to people working together to build stronger communities. The social needs of the people are more important than material goods. This concept has evolved over time to mean the power of social networks or who you know. This cannot be underestimated. In a recent conversation about an up-and-coming company, one of the executives told me they get thousands of resumes a day. I asked how they determined which were worth looking at or interviewing, and he said, "There is no way to tell. The only way you could get in is by creating a relationship with someone else in the company. It's all about your network."

Symbolic capital is an interesting one, but relevant here because it applies to historic value or mystique. Many of the wealthiest families in history still have symbolic capital as a part of their heritage. It opens doors even when they are penniless. You can create your own symbolic value through personal branding and your legacy.

Cultural capital refers to non-financial assets that can promote social mobility and gain economic support. Pierre Bourdieu, a French sociologist, talked about capital as a form of exchange. His theory applies to all goods and services without distinction as being a form of capital that can exchanged for the other. Any forms of capital that "present themselves as rare and worthy of being sought after" are part of the capital market system of exchange. This includes accumulated knowledge, such as education, vocation, skills, and training. Cultural: embodied (beliefs/character instilled), institutional (educated), objectified (collected arts).

Cultural capital also refers to attitudes and beliefs. These embodied forms of cultural capital have to do with your character and your way of thinking according to Bourdieu. This is very important!

When you think of capital and capital markets, consider what governs the world we live in. There are economic, cultural, and social capital aspects. The capital markets have often been referred to as a wheel because they are in constant flux, each moving and exchanging one for the other. Consider what greases the cogs on the wheel and nature's checks and balances. Economics takes into account money; social capital considers our network, while cultural capital consists of what we know, our education, and vocation. It is only natural that we should consider personal capital as another spoke in the capital wheel. This capital drives, balances, and jockeys for position in the capital markets. How much you have of one determines how much you can gain of another. You can obtain these forms of capital by earning them, joining forces with others who possess them, hiring them, marrying them, purchasing them, and a myriad of other ways.

Catherine Hakim, professor of Sociology at the prestigious London School of Economics, coined the phrase "Erotic Capital" in her recent book of the same name. Professor Hakim's exploration of the social consequences—and potential—of erotic capital is influential. Her conclusion is one that is so controversial most reviewers appear not to have read it. To her credit, she unemotionally slices through it all, addressing the basis of supply and demand as the solution and only one way women will reach economic equality. In Hakims theory, she talks of erotic capital consisting primarily of visual beauty, sexual attractiveness, and presentation. There is a great deal of evidence that women who leverage their erotic capital do so in exchange for more economic, social, and cultural capital. The world was in an uproar recently when it was discovered many young women strip and sell sex or other related goods or services to pay for their college tuitions. It's ironic that it makes more economical sense than working at Starbucks. Hakim is an advocate of women using their erotic capital to gain economic leverage, but not in the way I have outlined in this book.

Stepping beyond the external aspects of the visual impression and impulsive desires, we move into behaviors and beliefs. We fold them into our total persona, creating our personal power. We have the ability to change and direct our thoughts and develop new behaviors and turn them into habits, becoming stronger, more resilient people. Stephen Covey, Hank Fieger, Abraham Maslow, David Richo, and many others have shown people their personal ability to change behaviors and attitudes for more success, both personally and professionally. Sometimes a change comes in a short realization, others need to be acted out until they become a natural part of who we are and the way we see things changes.

Erotic capital can certainly create traction between social, economic, and cultural capital. My thoughts and experience, however, show that the idea of sex is far more valuable than the act itself. I am also a firm believer in high ROI and long-term emotional health, so for this to really work, aspects of personal capital must be developed in a diversified way and leveraged through their lifetime. It's clear that sex sells when you consider the advertising world and symbolic capital. Beauty is a billion dollar industry, and underneath the concept of beauty, it is really all about attraction and how sexy (valuable) we will be/feel, and how we will attract that spouse, date, mate, job, feeling, sensation, or love we crave. But this is not limited to sexual allure nor should it be.

Our personal capital is best used to attract what we want, acquire what we need, and leverage what we have to build the personal and professional lifestyle that fulfills us.

Use FLIRTonomics to increase your level of effectiveness and engagement to its full potential and access more economic capital, human capital (education, vocational skills, training), and social capital (expand your network and reach). FLIRT creates movement in the other forms of capital.

CHAPTER 3

Investing in Your Personal Capital
In Two Parts

The leadership instinct you are born with is the backbone. You develop the funny bone and the wishbone that go with it.
~ *Elaine* Agather

FLIRTonomics Fact:

*Flirting is more valuable than sex.
The public exchange through flirting
creates a positive energetic flow between
two people in a moment of connection
and understanding.*

It is important to maintain and invest in your personal asset portfolio. The navigation tools for survival are inside you; this is your 401k plan for life. You are given one "vehicle" (your physical body), and there are no trade-ins *(sometimes an upgrade)*. If you have even spoken with an investment advisor, then you are probably familiar with the terms "diversification," "asset allocation," and "rebalancing." When you invest for retirement, you are advised to keep a diversified portfolio of age-appropriate investments. Age-appropriateness is about risk-reward balance. In theory, we can tolerate more risk when we are young or less conservative. Apply this concept to your personal assets, and consider yourself a diversified portfolio of attributes. When we are young, our beauty and physical fitness may be our strong assets. As we mature, our social grace, style, and humor will pay long-term dividends.

Consider the economics of fear and FLIRTing. We have less fear of flirting and social engagement when we are young, then social stigmas creep in with our hormone development. We may begin to worry about what people will think or social labels. As women, we have a natural vested interest in "community," so we naturally worry about things that might disrupt that sense of balance. We learn to navigate social relations and intentions and take those skills into the workforce.

WHAT HAPPENS OVER TIME
WITHOUT ATTENTION

FLIRTing in our 20's

Our social training has now been solidified, and we are often out in the workforce and/or looking for a mate. We operate from a competitive perspective, rooted in the fear that there is not enough. The thing is, positive energy creates more for everyone. Your attitude about friendly engagement needs to be open to be successful. There are too many languages to learn to be closed off to those of your own age group, culture, and sex, and those of older age categories with different life experiences, stories, and careers.

FLIRTing in our 30's-40's

Socially, it has been on the decline. If we have now completely removed flirting from our lives, we may, and many do, find ourselves feeling flat and unimaginative. We may lack the type of engagement from our peers and even our spouse to feel good about ourselves. Things may become routine, which can spur us to end or damage our relationships in a subconscious attempt to drive the life-force back into ourselves. Perhaps you have heard or even said the following statements:

"I'm not going to dress up because I'm not trying to meet anyone."

Well, okay, but you are meeting me for drinks, and it would be more fun if you dressed as if you cared. And you might feel more attractive if you put some effort into your presentation… But can I say this? Well, I just did. Frankly, you might enjoy yourself more if it looked as if you were open to positive interactions.

"My husband is a jerk. I'm not going to have sex with him because he didn't call before he got home and he is not pleased with my spending."

This is my favorite because it drives a deep wedge between couples. They want to deprive the other of intimacy and connection, so they hurt themselves first in the process. I never really understood that because it compounds misunderstandings and is so incredibly, painfully lonely. It opens a crevasse, and it grows wider at an unpredictable pace. My recommendation is to never go to bed angry, connect often, and resolve quickly. Let your guard down!

PART ONE:
Your Internal & External Body

From the Outside: Your Personal Regime

When you diversify your investments, you protect your long-term health.

Diversification of your efforts depends on the culture and structure of the area where you live. In some contexts, beauty and social grace may have more value than intimacy or fertility, while in other cultures, it could be the opposite. Each is important and must be weighed together and adjusted when they get out of balance. Diversification between economic, social, erotic, and human capital will help you protect your assets and relationships. It keeps them growing and moving. Remember, we are talking about change and movement because we are increasing awareness and growth in the areas of our personal capital. Vitality is the key to long life and long relationships.

People sometimes make the mistake, particularly when getting older, in spending gobs of economic capital on one area of their personal portfolio (beauty, skin lifts, tummy tucks, etc.), while others are unattended. It does not matter how beautiful you look if you are not well developed from the inside out.

Your vitality and inner energy is one of the most important aspects of your FLIRTonomics.

Beauty

Personal beauty starts with your face and what you see in the faces of others. The eyes tell a great deal about a person, and the skin is a tattle-tale of our internal health. Learn to apply personal care to your face and different types of regimens for skin care, from pores to hair follicles. Learn the history of skin care, the values different cultures have placed on the face, and how your diet, emotions, and energy are translated through your skin. You will learn how to read the lines in others and how to have a deeper understanding of what is going on with others by what you see on their face and in their skin.

"Beauty delights the senses and pleasures the mind," according to one definition. You may be born with it, or born with less. Still, many women and men present the idea of beauty by enhancing certain attributes or lessening others. These days, we can also increase our external beauty with capital. We can buy beauty or beautiful features with lip enhancers, facelifts, eyelid lifts, eyebrow tattoos, lip liner tattoos, facial peels, dermabrasion, and many other procedures. We can also enhance it with other aspects of our FLIRTonomics, our thoughts, and our actions.

You can increase facial beauty by keeping your skin exceptionally clean and clear. Proper hygiene, nutrition, and exercise are fundamental to internal and external health. This radiates beauty. We can enhance our features with cosmetics and more serious treatments if we choose. Focusing on one attribute, such as facial beauty, is like investing your entire portfolio in high-risk stocks when you are 50 years old. Your personal development portfolio should be invested in a diversified way, accommodating the scope of your life and attributes that pay dividends.

Develop a Beauty Regime

When you apply self-care, your face and your body will become more beautiful. Keep it simple. Depending on the type of skin you have and any level of corrective measures you need to take, it should not take longer than 15 to 60 minutes a day, including exercise. Some of us need to do a little more, others a little less.

Start the day with a glass of hot or cold lemon water. Drink this every day, and it will increase the body's ability to shed dead skin cells and keep new cells regenerating. Vitamin C is important for the skin. You can use vitamin C creams and tinctures, but consuming it will let the entire body benefit from its cleansing properties.

Supporting the body's ability to cleanse is key to radiating beauty on your face. Doing a minor monthly cleanse for your skin where you consume only broths and liquids for a 24-hour period will keep your skin healthy and increase your vitality. A purged body feels spritely and energetic.

- Facial exercises are very effective if you are over 30 years old

- Stay out of direct sunlight for extended periods of time

- Cleanse your skin, but do not overdo it

- What goes on in your body is reflected in your face
- Your internal organs are reflected in your face
- Your facial expression is very important
- If you have a negative facial expression as your relaxed state, ask yourself what is going on to create it or what old habits ingrained those lines
- Change your facial expression, use photographs and video to see what others see
- The face is full of muscles; you can retrain your face to have new expressions even in its relaxed state
- Reward yourself for new expressions by accepting others' positive reaction to you with gratitude

Your Skin

Your skin covers your entire body and should include your nails, as well. Sloughing off dry, old cells allows your new skin to continue its rejuvenation process freely. Keep your hands and nails well manicured and cared for. You do not need any capital to do this other than a nail file, clippers, and some lotion. A clear polish is enough. Clean, clear, and simple is the best choice to start with. From there, you can move into any direction that will serve your next meeting or appointment.

Physical Health & Fitness

This is defined by the way you move, your body language, your behaviors, or mannerisms (not manners). A healthy body is sexually attractive and creates a pallet for the lws of attraction to take place. Your physical health is defined by what you eat, your personal hygiene, smell, and physical appearance. Your body weight is a key factor in this, obviously. Physical fitness can take place at any age, and it is also determined by body type and diet.

Many people avoid exercise because they think of it as too much work. You do not need to exercise strenuously to stay fit and keep weight off. You need to move your body! Most people gain weight because of what they eat and over-eat. Sticking with unprocessed foods and away from breads does the trick for me. Everyone is different, though, and noticing what makes you feel good and what makes you feel guilty, obsessive, slow, tired, sluggish, or less than energetic is something you should pay attention to. Stay away from food and things that make you feel less than fabulous. Your body is talking to you. Extreme measures breed failure and resentment. Do not be too hard on yourself. Happiness is a great diet. Keeping fit involves two key elements: Moving your body and putting good things in it—not doing either one in excess.

Keeping fit is key to the economics of FLIRT because being physically attractive with vital energy makes you FEEL attractive and it gives you leverage. It communicates to everyone that you care about your appearance and your health. This is even more important as you get older.

Ways to Keep Fit

1. Stretching
2. Yoga
3. Walking
4. Joining a gym
5. Joining a fitness group
6. Eating right for your body type
7. Lifting weights

Social Grace

Your social grace is defined by your social skills of engagement and etiquette. What language are you speaking with your charm, manners, flirtations, laughter, and the skill with which you put people at ease? Do you hug them, kiss their cheek, or touch them in any way when you meet? This is critical to manners and to connecting. Even the traditional handshake should not be missed and must be done correctly. The warmer you are, the more warmth and comfort will come back. You must respect the culture in which you are in, yet sometimes it is good to go with personal judgment. In the U.S., we have developed a culture that discourages touching, which is probably the most unhealthy aspect affecting our culture today. Touch and connect with signifying manners and respect.

Vitality

Your energy or vitality is what you bring to the occasion. Positive energy is defined by what you give off and share through enthusiasm and willingness. Effort creates leadership. One person who is willing to step forward first with a positive attitude can shift the vital energy of a group and of an experience for everyone. Noticing how you feel is the key to your inner vitality. This starts with noticing what you put in your body. How it affects your energy is the first step toward getting healthy and bringing up your vital energy.

The other aspect about vital energy is directly linked to your attitude. Positive thoughts create positive energy. You can control what you think. If you do not believe it, ask yourself if you listen to yourself or others. If you can follow their words, their stories, and their language, then you are thinking about what they are saying. They are your guides. You can be your own guide. Remove the self-talk by focusing your attention on something outside of yourself. If this is a challenge, follow my step-by-step guide and you will stop that cycle.

Start now by making a list of five things you are grateful for.

1. _____
2. _____
3. _____
4. _____
5. _____

Self-Presentation

Your self-presentation is defined by what people perceive when they see you. It is visual and has to do with your body language in posture and movement, as well as colors, style, and accessories for the occasion. Are you prepared; are you clean and respectful of the occasion and the company? Your body posture is a huge factor in swaying people's perception of you and your ability to communicate personally and publically before they see your face and can determine facial expression or attractiveness. They will already have a sense of your attractiveness and who you are before they engage with you. Your voice and use of language is another fundamental factor.

It may seem shallow, but it is factual that accessories, brands, and colors affect other people's interpretation of you because they are signifiers before they get to know you. These signifiers can be positive or negative if not used in the appropriate context. If you are over-dressed or under-dressed, it can be a signal of disrespect or self-adoration. Wearing color combinations that suit your skin and body type, as well as clothing that fits well, is more important than brand-identity. Sometimes people adhere to brand identity when they are lacking in some other form of personal asset development. What is presented maintains relevance in the context it is used. For example, young girls with expensive brands signify they are "taken care of" buy someone else. Older women with the same brands signify they have "earned" it. Consistency in a color palette will make your shopping easy and getting dressed painless.

Our body movements synchronize with whoever we interact. When there is good synchronization, positive feels emerge. When there is a lack of synchronization, it leads to feelings of discomfort. Charismatic people have an open body language. Their hands and palms face out, with arms slightly open as is to embrace the world—and the world embraces them in return. Crossed arms shows indifference or a dislike of the person who is being interacted with, as well as being a protective measure for them. When I see people crossing their arms after a meeting, it is usually a defensive reaction to "protect: themselves.

Leaning forward while standing or sitting demonstrates interest. Leaning slightly backward or sideways with loose hands can demonstrate a sense of equality or of regarding the counterpart to be of lower status. This posture is often used by men in the company of women.

Your facial expression will allow you to master body language. Smile if it kills you! Notice your types of smiles by using mirrors or photographs. Practice loving kindness with your smile and facial expressions. The act of smiling will manifest the appropriate feelings in you to go with it.

EXERCISE

Notice people's body language. Practice different postures in your interactions with others.

Make notes:

INVESTING IN YOUR PERSONAL CAPITAL IN TWO PARTS

Intimacy Skills

Intimacy skills are wonderful tools to have, and they help maintain long-term relationships. They are internal and external, involving your thoughts, your emotions, and your actions. There is a difference between skills, and tricks geared toward getting results are not the same. Skills are flexible and attentive to the other person; tricks are simply self-indulgent acts. In intimacy, there is a strive for a certain attentiveness and awareness. There are behaviors that can enhance reaching those levels of communication and engagement. There is no "goal" in mind, just openness to discovery. With so many social stigmas around behaviors that can develop intimacy and sexuality, you may feel like you need to teach yourself. It is no wonder so many people have difficulty maintaining relationships and feel vulnerable and uncomfortable in intimate situations.

Intimacy and being competent in intimate situations keeps your relationship stable and happy. Generosity and gratitude are key ingredients. They are important to maintaining and developing relationships and being vulnerable yourself. Intimacy has its place and levels. It is not just about sexuality, but also about how close you can become emotionally with others, while being open to sharing experiences with them. Most often, sexual skills are known only between partners. Your skills in the bedroom are not consummated solely in the ultimate act of connection between two people. Intimacy and self-expression shared through eroticism and play have ramifications in every other area of our relationships. The better we are at communicating in intimate situations, the better we are at communicating through difficulty in other areas of our lives. Sexual skills are a matter of experience, but not from performing a sexual act. They come from your ability to listen and respond physically, creatively, and imaginatively as an act of communication. The most successful individuals possessing high levels of personal capital excel as much in communication as they do in professional and communication.

It is an opportunity to open internally and share your insides, literally and figuratively, with another human being. The skill of being able to look completely at your partner, be present in the moment, blocking all else or any other thought, becomes a spiritual experience.

Nurture

The ability to nurture through care, comforting, and cooking is an aspect of personal capital and a form of expression and communication. Unfortunately, nurture has fallen by the wayside in much of American culture, and despite endless cooking shows on TV, we continue to grow fatter and fatter, which is a reflection of our unfulfilled needs. The care and act of nurturing is food for soul. Surprisingly, cooking is also a form of cultural capital. The more skilled you are in the kitchen, the more skilled you are in taste, organization, and aesthetic beauty. Cooking with a partner can be a sensual, connecting activity that deepens your relationships with friends and loved ones. We can develop our femininity be developing our ability to nurture others.

Fertility of the Mind

Our body's fertility is a transitory thing when you consider the act of child bearing and the period in which we are able to do it. As women, we usually hit a transition point in our 40's. But fertility of the mind is a continual state and process. FLIRT your creativity by seeing the world differently than most people. It is a great way to engage in conversation with just about anyone. When you begin to notice things around you, how they are organized, what this means, or if it seems out of place, commenting on it can bring humor or surprise.

Fertility of the mind can be fed throughout your life with creative or learning projects, like art or cooking. It is cultural in nature and active. Reading, writing, learning, and sharing are ways to keep the stimulation going and keep your mind healthy throughout your life. Stagnation is never a good cure for anything. Staying fertile in your mind is the fountain of youth. It is what all your FLIRT investment amounts to as you mature.

What Goes into Your Body Matters

Diet

By this, we mean what you eat, not food deprivation. This is a package deal, and how you think is the most important component to staying fit. The primary thing is to tell yourself how fabulous you feel and keep checking in with yourself. Notice how certain foods make you feel. Are you tired after eating or energized? Do some things make you sleepy?

It has been said that you can keep fit by your consumption alone. Eating the foods that work well for your body type is the first step. You do not need to go out and buy a diet book to understand or learn this. Start removing foods that provide any negative reaction in energy or self-talk. Your food provides the energy you need throughout the day. If food is not giving you health and energy, eliminate it. This is critical to your vitality and the energy you share with others. What goes in your body should be of the best quality you can get. The least you can do for yourself is stick to unprocessed foods.

Are you regular in your daily maintenance? Many people are not regular because they are not eating foods appropriate for their digestive ability. Take it easy on yourself. Be kind to your body and treat it as you would a child or a plant. It is extremely important to facilitate your daily process.

EXERCISE

List foods and their effect on your mood & energy (positive, negative, neutral) and what time of day they were consumed. Foods consumed at different times of day will have different results because of your natural daily rhythms.

Food	Mood	Energy	Time of Day

Vitamins Help

It may be obvious to some, but even I initially refused vitamins. They were so strong they made me sick. Since I have always been a healthy eater, I thought I could get my nutritional value from my food. Vitamins during pregnancy made a marked difference, and at many times thereafter when stress began to accumulate. A multivitamin or vitamins tailored to your needs is very helpful in maintaining energy and, therefore, weight. The results have been surprising for me in terms of reducing cravings around sugar.

PART TWO:
Social Fluency = Behaviors Build Charisma

Social Fluency

Social fluency is a set of skills allowing us to communicate effectively in different social environments. They are behaviors and mannerisms, where other aspects of charisma and femininity have to do with self-care, beauty regimes, and internal health.

As the term suggests, your fluency is a language dependent on your expertise and the nuances of the culture you are in. Being socially fluent involves other communication tools, including body language, assertiveness, a sense of humor, and the ability to put others at ease. Our skill can break tension, navigate conversation, and create mental flexibility. Manners and social skills are key attributes of FLIRTonomics. Your awareness of how others are feeling around you helps you adapt your behavior and interaction to theirs. Notice when you are engaging with people from different cultures, religions, and backgrounds than your own. You never want to lose a sense of ease, but you also want to adopt posture and contact that is appropriate to the people with whom you are engaging. Social grace is etiquette, manners, behaviors, body language, and attributes where you mirror, emulate, or imitate body language. Flexibility in our mindset allows us to navigate conversations with skill. Once we are trained in the skill of conversation, we will enjoy them more and those who engage with us will have more positive residual feelings. This takes practice.

When you eat properly at the table, set it well and place your fork and knife at 4 o'clock when finished, and you will be exhibiting more manners than 90% of people you encounter. Despite the lack of knowledge, your deliberateness in how you place food in your mouth, chewing with your mouth closed, and not talking while chewing will be noticeable and noted subconsciously by your dinner partners.

Manners are a form of communication, and etiquette is a form of class. Get it, learn it, and use it! Here are some of the basics you can consider in business and personal communication.

1. Communicate effectively

2. Dress for the meeting

3. Wait for the other person to speak

4. Write thank you notes and keep ongoing communications

5. Remember birthdays and holidays specific to your clients and friends

6. Have good manners at the table, and when entering and exiting a meeting

7. Set an example

8. Provide guidance in areas other than financial

Then, you can do a few additional things:

1. Consider people's family and personal lives

2. Offer advice and contacts to help them realize dreams

3. Communicate there is no time like now to live well

4. Bring enthusiasm and stories to people's lives

5. Instill personal confidence

Communicating effectively has several components. It is a process where information is exchanged and understood. We communicate through what we look like, our body language, our method/pace of speaking, our choice of words, and the actions we express in front of others. When good communication happens, information is exchanged, processed, and questions are answered. As humans, we can't help but ask questions, even subconsciously, every time we engage with someone or notice them. We deal in the context of speaker/sender, talker/receiver, and actor/observer.

We send messages through:

- The spoken word
- Body language
- Eye contact
- Written word
- Tonality
- Touch

We receive messages through:

- Observing
- Listening
- Touch
- Our impressions or energy

This is translated through:

- Our emotional response
- Other reactions
- Our intellectual response/inclination

You are always communicating, so it's good to consider what that message is. With enough practice, behaviors evolve to principles–they become a part of you. You can learn behaviors and combine them with your existing values. Your dress and mannerisms convey a lot before you start speaking. Bring energy to meetings, being conscious of it as a value-add, and it will open doors. Curb your energy relative to the person you are communicating with. Yes, this demands constant attention and noticing others behaviors and expressions. Consider yourself a student of human behavior.

There is an art to making conversation, the first step in communicating outside of the eye contact and body language that tells you to communicate. How you say something is often more important than what you say. It is not always necessary to jump immediately into deep conversation, but sometimes it is. Casual, empty conversation is a bore for everyone, especially when you are unable to find the triggers that engage. By listening, you can learn how to allow the other person to feel like they are opening the channel. Then, allow them to reach in themselves and share what is really on their minds. Anyone who is at ease in conversation is an asset in business and personal relationships. It is important to be polite and to care about the exchange, or it will not be meaningful later. This is a clue for someone who is not well intentioned. If they are not paying attention to you, their eyes leaving your face often, it shows they may be uncomfortable or disingenuous. You should be well-informed on a variety of topics. You must be interested to be interesting. When you are interested in many topics, you can engage with knowledge and make a positive contribution to a conversation while you listen. Keeping the conversation moving smoothly is a skill, so look for transitions to suit the person or group you are engaging with. Include others and specifically direct conversation to include the reserved people in the group.

Eye contact is critical to good conversation and to developing trust. Always look people in the eye, note their eye color, the texture, if there is any allergenic response going on, yellowness, or any other aspect that would indicate personal health and attention. Look beyond the ordinary because the face can reveal so much. Looking into the eyes (not too deeply or too long, because that can be interpreted as too intimate) can tell you about how the person is feeling emotionally and physically. It is also a matter of quality attention versus cursory. Engage and lock quickly to connect.

In conversation, do not be contradictory or correct grammar unless there is a misunderstanding that is occurring because of the misuse of a term, grammar, or context. If there seems to be confusion, help to clarify it immediately by repeating the question correctly to get clarification, understanding, and agreement. Do not reveal personal attributes about a person that you know or notice in front of others. Always compliment and uplift the conversation with the positive. Do not gossip!

There still are topics to avoid, unless someone really wants to know:

- General gripes about public policy based on politics
- Personal health details in a group
- Sexual conversation
- Heated topics you can tell will dominate emotional behaviors

- Gossip, gossip, gossip (maintain integrity, privacy, and confidentiality)
- Personal problems
- Age and income

Although small talk might seem tedious, think of it this way: Small talk does not have to be about the weather, it can be about some news event or an uplifting fact. From here, it begins to move away from "small talk," but is still considered light, engaging conversation that can be silly, fun, or enlightening. This is not about how much you know, it's about engaging with who you know and meeting more people.

How do you make small talk? Just think of writing. Who, what, when, where, and why are great conversation openers...how is a great conversation continuer. Make sure you ask open-ended questions. Follow the 80/20 rule throughout your process. Give them 80% of the floor, you can take 20%.

Some good conversation openers are:

"Wow, this is a great venue. How long has this organization been doing it? What brought you here?"

"I'm so curious about everyone here, how do you know the hosts?"

"How are you enjoying this event? Have you been to many others? What type of connections have you made?"

"I love your outfit. The colors look great on your skin. How did you learn to shop like that?"

These are simple because they can die off quickly if you do not get to meaningful content as a result. You must keep the conversation going or pick up on a signal to get lost. (Crossed arms or turning away from you would convey that message.) Do not ask for professional advice at a group event. It is rude and may disrespect the value of what your receiver does for a living. Also, be careful about overly friendly banter that has

69

innuendos; use some to create fun. Do not banter in a way that can be misunderstood as a "come-on>" I can tell you from experience that it is not helpful.

How to keep yourself stimulating and interesting in conversation

- Keep up-to-date on current events.
- Subscribe to *Wall Street Journal* and the *New York Times* on line.
- Keep yourself busy doing activities.
- Use social media to keep up with what is going on with people and friends.
- Clip international and global news to find direction in nationwide economic reactions.
- Read articles and watch clips, etc., to keep up with trends.
- Do research daily on topics of interest.
- Pass along good information to others who would find it relevant.
- Steer clear of jokes or chain letters. No one has time to waste unless it is extraordinary.
- Read relevant material on industries before attending related events.
- Notice everything people do and what they are paying attention to, then tease them a bit to let them know you are paying attention.
- Pay attention to conversation, and when you are tired, excuse yourself.

Communication takes more than one participant. When you pay attention, listen, and engage, you will find people respond to you quickly and positively. Simple manners seem to have deteriorated, so the simple act of saying "thank you," pointedly and "please" are great ways to improve your communications.

They should be used in every context, as well as other ways of letting people know you have recognized their efforts. It is a way of showing kindness and giving something back.

When you are speaking in conversation and publically, your delivery is very important. When I'm on the phone, I can immediately tell, based on how someone sounds, their pace of speech, response rate, and tone, if I want to meet them at all, and if so, how long the meeting should last. The level of their enthusiasm can change with yours and with the use of certain language. Test it on the phone where you are not distracted with the visual.

I was an intensely shy person when growing up, particularly in the realm of public speaking or coming into a room full of people where they might all focus their attention on me at once. In fact, I was so shy, that once when some people ran up to me as I walked into a restaurant, I stopped breathing and passed out. The ambulance came, and I was rushed to the hospital because they could not figure out what happened. Thankfully, those days are long gone. I trained myself out of it to some degree, and working in financial sales forced me to overcome it. At first, my knees knocked, and my heart still flutters, but I can attest: if I can do it, you can, too!

To be successful in business and attract clients, you need to learn to present yourself and your story in an articulate, meaningful, and powerful way. You practice every day that you speak to someone about what you do, whether it is in person or on the phone. How you speak and articulate your words is important. How you pace with the person you are speaking to is also important. When you are too excited, talking too fast, you are focused on yourself. You are not paying attention to your receiver. You need to gage your excitement with theirs.

The Way You Talk

Thirty-eight percent of the way you influence others has to do with how you use your voice. Men are more influenced by what they see; women are more influenced by what they hear.

Men and women are influenced by each, just weighted in the way I described. These statistics are found in dating, as well as in business and personal studies. A lower-toned voice can sometimes make it difficult to be understood or heard in a crowd.

Listen to yourself. Are you loud or a mumbler? Are you a fast talker, slow talker, lisper, or screecher? Do you sound like you look? Just as the quality of your clothes pleases the eye and your handshake pleases the touch, your voice should also please the ear. Record yourself talking about different things. You can learn a lot. I have used my voice to navigate some very threatening situations by calming and soothing when I was in my twenties, and I was able to keep myself in one piece. The voice is a very powerful tool.

Record your voice when reading and then talking. Record yourself in conversation with a friend. Note if you sound interested or disinterested, controlled or loose in your speech. Voice lessons or video recordings are excellent ways to get feedback and learn about your voice. We work with people in our photo-therapy classes to show what they look like, sound like, and demonstrate with their own body language. People are as surprised as I was when I started it, and it does make a world of difference in personal body communication awareness.

Aspects of Your Voice

Pitch—Your pitch should be in the mid-range—not too high and not too low. Newscasters, radio announcers, and TV personalities are very good at this, and you can learn from them. Keep the high shrills out of your voice. If you need to, get a voice coach. Excitement can be done without the high shrill. Personally, it hurts most people's ears, and they will recoil from people with high-pitched voices. Avoid monotone.

Speed—Do not talk too fast or too slow. Keep it even and measure the number of words per minute. People will associate you with different areas of the country based on your speed. You are supposed to vary the rate based on the excitement level of the point you are making. If you are out of synch, you may create distrust.

Inflection—This is how you add emotion to your words and to your story. First notice your voice, then add the inflection where you want to convey your personal feelings to the story or conversation. Help your listener understand the areas you are passionate about. When you fail to do this, you fail to provide meaning to the words you are saying when all they have are their ears to provide them with information. You can say the same thing, like "what did you do today?" with anger, with love, with curiosity, with judgment, and get the appropriate reactions for each.

Rhythm—The rate your voice rises or falls and the speed that you speak in has a rhythm. The rhythm is what makes it easy or difficult to listen to you and follow your conversation. It also allows the receiver to recall what you said more easily.

Resonance—This is considered to be fullness of voice or echo, reverberation. When you inhale deeply before speaking and articulate openly with a wider mouth, your voice will have more resonance.

Volume—Practice soothing with your voice; make it a pleasure for people to hear or listen to you. When people speak too loudly, it can be as hard to collect all the information as it is when they speak too softly.

Keep working on your vocabulary and use the dictionary often to find new words or ways of saying things with more meaning. Expanding your vocabulary will give you more freedom of speech. Do not forget to use the thesaurus, as well. Dictionary.com can be set up to provide you with a new word on your mobile device every day. No longer will your studies for the ACT or SAT have to represent your highest level of vocabulary excellence!

Practice what you are going to say. Get your 10-second elevator pitch down. Rehearse your speech in front of the mirror or in front of a friend. Make sure your notes are guiding with clues that lead, not using too many words so you lose your place. Breathe deeply before you present or enter any social event. I sometimes start my breathing exercises hours before to keep myself calm and focused, depending on the type of event. Visualize your success at the end of your speech or meeting. Consider potential questions and adjust your presentation accordingly so you can easily visualize the response you desire.

When you are the one doing introductions at an event, keep it brief and use names and the name of the venue. Give thanks and make the introduction with a positive statement about the speaker. Note his or her past qualifications and experience, but don't use their stories or past speeches. Approach the stage or podium with energy and a swift intention. When you are the presenter, keep things focused, add some levity, and keep palms open. Relax and take deep breaths as you can, even during the speech, if needed. Do not reveal your nervousness or detract attention from your presentation or audience expectation.

The Way You Walk

Learning how to walk in a certain way, depending on the circumstances, is a message in itself. It tells a lot about you and your situation. It has kept me from being harassed or stopped in the street by anyone who might want to take advantage of me. Never walk in a diminished way if you do not want to be seen as a victim or prey.

As the costume designer in the movie PanAm, where she used original uniforms and photographs from archives and flight attendants in researching the styles used in the show, Ann Crabtree says, "One thing I continue to tell our actors and extras is to hold your head high, shoulders back, no slouching." "It's a rethink of how one maneuvers, physically, in the world. We've been taught in the '90s and 2000s to be childlike, waifs, slack in our stance. All of that ... would be a telltale sign of holding onto 2011, which I hope doesn't slip into view."

It's a public revelation on how women have been socialized to act and be small. We can empower ourselves by standing up straight and having great posture. Great posture does more than just look good and make your clothes hang better. Standing up straight allows the body to take in more oxygen, actually making you stronger and increasing your vitality. It aligns your body and lets your bones and muscles fall into place. This makes you FEEL better; people who see you will be attracted to you. People want to be near people who feel good because they instinctually know it will make them feel good, too. Humans are highly vibrational beings, and we thrive on each other's energy. Our posture and energetic presence can shape every interaction we have, either positively or negatively.

In business, be quick to take a step, keep your feet measured together and posture erect. Focus your attention on the person you are approaching, and allow your entire body language to communicate your purpose. There is no flailing of limbs; elbows and hips are straight and tucked in. No loose swing. In casual events where people are observing you, try crossing the room with a long, slightly casual stride. It is also even and measured, but somewhat self conscious. Visualize which people will be the ones who watch.

When walking down the street, especially at night or alone, always walk erect, even paced, but with agility. Convey that you can move very fast; your gait and posture should indicate that. If it appears to be a potentially dangerous area, visualize a possible situation and put your inner strength forward. People will sense that you are not an easy target. When you do not want to be interrupted, you will have a different gait and body language. Again, your attention is usually on your subject; allow zero peripheral vision to intrude or distract. Aware people will get the message and wait; others will realize they can't keep up as you move swiftly and aggressively with purpose to the goal of getting to one person or to an area of the room. Keep your focus, especially if it is easy for you to get distracted.

My usual approach is a nice easy gait; my hands hang gently at my sides with my palms open and facing forward. I am receptive. My mouth is gentle and lips relaxed, with a soft smile at the edge, again "open.: Keep your eyes moving and generally look about to see others and catch the eye of as many people as you can. Say hello with your eyes, your mouth (mouth the words if you are moving), and nod. If you are close to people, offer a passing compliment on something about them or that they are doing. This is positive gift you can give with intention.

The Way You Listen

The best thing you can do to increase your communication skills is to listen. You do this with intention and attention. Offer space between your discussion and allow the other person to speak and add content. Communicate through your body language that you are listening. This means eye contact or eyes resting on the face of the person you are listening to. It means facing your body all of the way toward them. Do not allow your eyes to dart around or your head to turn. If you do, they will be distracted from what they are saying and look where you are looking. Do not look down at your phone or purse unless they do. You have great control in the conversation, and you can decide when it is over. This is a great gift you can give, and you can do it anytime.

Your Written Communications

It is important to offer the correct types of correspondence. Teens these days do not seem to know where to place the return and sender's address. Your stationary is an extension of your business brand. Informal means personal to you; formal means including your business letterhead. Informal note cards are for jotting down quick notes or thoughts to clients and friends.

Touching Others

I am a firm believer in the influence of touch, but you MUST be aware of the person you are communicating with. Certain types of touching can be construed as a come-on. Even a man's touch on the arm or elbow of a woman can be taken as an indication of interest in the United States, but that does not mean you should not do it. Kissing on the cheek is acceptable in Europe and should be implemented here. It breaks the ice and is warmer than a handshake. Always shake hands during an introduction, but please do so correctly. A good handshake involves the whole hand, palms touching, thumbs locked. Beware of people who shake hands carelessly or who try to hurt you with their handshake. There are many of these types, unfortunately. If they hurt you without intention, then they are simply careless, and that is also some information for you to note. If it seems appropriate, close your left hand over theirs in the handshake for a warmer, more sincere connection. Do not engage in air kissing or restrained hugging. It is uncomfortable and shows a lack of sincerity.

"The tactile feeling of touching ourselves, touching our own truth, letting ourselves be moved is really connecting. Every single moment is an opportunity to connect fully and deeply to the core with the sun, with a friend, with your child, with a business associate, with your beloved. We're the only ones in the way of holding this barrier up; when we let ourselves be touched, then we can be touched."
~Allana Pratt, Family & Relationship Expert,
Speaker, Coach, Author

If you touch someone and it is not well received, apologize immediately, with calmness and sincerity. This has never happened to me, but I have used my hands for healing all my life. My hyper-awareness would probably dictate I touch more often than I do. Women seem to be the ones who touch men inappropriately as much or more than men do these days. A woman who reaches out and pats or squeezes a man's belly when he says he has been working out should be reprimanded. If a man did that to a woman, she would most likely be outraged.

I cannot stress enough that you pay attention. What is considered to be good etiquette in one country is not the same in another. Social etiquette, cultural etiquette, and business etiquette all have slightly different applications. Be aware of what they are and your position in the context of the meeting at the time. As you get to know the person better, you will move from one style to another.

Sometimes people use the tools incorrectly. For example, I met with a professional woman and talked with her about her client communications. She was in an industry that had been having difficulties and had branded herself as a product salesperson. Since the industry was having difficulty, when she called clients, they practically hung up on her, saying they did not want that right now. They did not take the time for "hellos," "how are yous," or any other personal dialogue. We talked about communicating with emails, cards, and finding out more about her clients, developing strategic partnerships, and even uncovered an area of expertise that was recession-proof where she could start making money immediately.

A few days after the meeting, I was surprised to receive a handwritten card from her stating her role as my strategic partner and advisor. First, I did not own anything her product could service. Second, I would have expected a thank you and perhaps a note of the direction she had decided to take, perhaps an offer of referral or even a question. But instead it was clear she had been given enough information to be dangerous, but not enough to be effective. Over the next three months, she figured out some aspects, but she needed a little more advice. Context and audience are incredibly important. You should never send a note to a prospect, assuming them to be a client. You can send them a note thanking them for the meeting and looking forward to the next steps that you set up at the end of the first meeting.

Body Language

I've discussed some aspects of body language and have made a practice of learning, understanding, and reading it. I began to do it at a young age and have continued to study it through film, media, business, cultural studies, travel, communication, experience, and observation. There are many exercises and experiments you can use to see if someone is following you or if you are following them. This is important to understand if you are in leadership roles or aspire to them. I work through many of these studies and experiments in my training courses. Body language is non-verbal communication telling us about the person who is doing the talking, as well as how others respond to them.

A few notes to observe:

Eye contact and gaze are important indicators. The length of time, exact focus, and direction the gaze comes from reveal sincerity, intention, objectives, and interest. The "eyebrow flash" is directive in signaling breaks in the conversation or turn-taking (who will speak next). Head movement, body movement, gestures, and posturing also convey underlying messages. Stance, proximity, and orientation are also indicators.

Your success in reading and utilizing body language is based on your ability to accurately observe others. As an exercise, go to a public place and pay attention to what people are doing. Do not let others notice you noticing. What are they looking at, interested in? What is their reaction when their appointment or date approaches them? How does their body language reflect their level of interest, excitement, distaste, or professionalism? How long is eye contact made? Is there physical contact, and in what context? Make notes and then evaluate what you learned. Try out some of the behaviors and gage the response. Note that it is important to allow people to be comfortable, but also to help them get comfortable. This will strengthen your relationships and understanding of other people. In meetings, note which direction your counterpart's legs are crossed. They will either be toward you or away from you. They indicate interest or disinterest. Arms crossed or open indicate the same thing. People have a very difficult time falsifying their body language and eye movements. The direction of their thoughts can be read on most people's faces. That is why it is so important for you to remain open. Openness in your body shows comfort and demonstrates a charismatic presence.

CASE STUDY
Social Gathering

"There are no good men to date anymore."

This was said to me at an elegant, well-heeled art opening by an attractive woman who sought me out. I was coming out of the kitchen when we had eye contact as I came through the door. I knew immediately that we would be talking, but I rounded the corner and started checking out some of the pieces on the wall. A few moments later, the women arrived by my side and we started to chat. She had dark hair, clean skin, was tall, and her body language told me she was seeking something. I turned to face her completely so I could see her face and hear what she had to say. She asked me what I did, and I told her I did strategic business consulting (more loudly) and was developing a training program (more softly) in the area of erotic capital. When she heard me say "erotic," she did a double-take and said, "What did you say?"

I laughed, leaned forward and said, very articulately and slowly, "Yes, I said, Er-raa-Tic," and burst out laughing. She began to laugh, too, and then burst out in a serious rush and said, "There are no men around here."

"What do you mean?" I replied, gazing about and extending my arm. "There are tons of amazing men here, including the artist host."

She looked around. There were many attractive men who were dressed well. The man I was with had disappeared, and I imagined him chatting up a woman in the kitchen or around the corner. I smiled at the thought, knowing how friendly he is.

"Well, how do you do that?" she asked.

I took a look at her, up and down, and said, "Let's start with the direction your feet are pointing. Mine are pointing straight at you because I am giving you all of my attention. Now one foot is pointed a bit away, so straighten your legs and feet and have them directed at me."

I reached out and touched her elbow. She straightened her feet.

"Now, let's look at your posture. Stand up straight, move your collar bone up and your shoulders back. I always let my hands fall gently at my side, palms facing slightly forward, open and receptive to whatever might come my way."

She looked at me, and said, "Oh, I am doing this." She clenched up her arms and hugged them back against her chest, elbows pointing toward me now, wrists back up by her collar bone.

"Yes," I said and took her things. Move your arms down, pull your energy down. Get it away from your neck and head. Pull it down and let it move down your arms."

She did as instructed and noted it did feel better. I explained to her that being open was about being able to receive whatever might come your way. It's being able to scoop up and embrace whatever the universe delivers to you.

Within a couple of minutes, a very handsome Stanford doctor walked up and started talking with her. It was quite amazing to see it work so quickly, but we had opened up the space to allow others to come in, and she had suddenly become approachable. I excused myself and found my friend in the kitchen—having collided with a glass of wine, he was washing his shirt. The rest of the evening, the woman had a line of men talking with her and was very engaged, enjoying herself.

Learning to speak body language is essential in making yourself approachable. People will see that before they can see your facial expression. Your attitude is one of the keystones for this process. Sloppy behavior indicates a sloppy attitude toward the person or group you are interacting with. When you care about yourself, people will respect you more. You must be your own living example of behavior and image. Mindfulness comes in self-presentation, attention, and how you focus it on someone else. The power of attraction starts with being attractive to yourself. Good manners are not distracting; they show a healthy mind and spirit.

CHAPTER 4

FLIRTing is Healthy Human Behavior

*"The most important thing in communication is to
hear what isn't being said."*
~Peter F. Drucker, Author

OUR BRAIN | OUR PERCEPTION |
OUR UNDERSTANDING | OUR CONNECTION

In the basest manner, flirting, charisma, social charm, and
attractiveness open doors that might not otherwise be opened.
This skill-set increases positive response to your presence,
increasing your personal general happiness, but more
importantly, it affects how you see the world, how the world
sees you, and how it responds to you. A powerful positive
response can change public policy or create economic
movement where money or goods change hands. It builds
relationships, expands social networks, and builds groups,
teams, and constituents. The kind of movement that allows
economic growth in any area you focus on can build social
awareness, increase loving kindness, and make you a better
parent, child, friend, and member of your community.
Fundamentally, it's the type of movement that changes our
level of cultural capital and makes us far wealthier in every
area of our lives.

FLIRTing has an element of laughter and humor. What
better way to maintain our vitality than to maintain our humor

and ability to laugh at ourselves and with others? Positive interactions throughout our day bring joy into our lives and the lives of others. It builds our "team" and expands our sense of belonging to the collective.

Studies in human brain cognition show that we have a unique way of relating to each other, differently than other animals. Developing empathic communication or compassionate communication is key to recognizing the needs of others and our own needs. We often shut our feelings down and because we lack an understanding of our own needs, we fail to have compassion for the needs of others. When we begin to notice and serve those needs in others, it causes us to realize our own needs.

THE HUMAN CONNECTION

The purpose here is to help you notice what you are doing, how people react to you, and learn how to speak their language so you can both be understood. You should use whatever methods you have in order to communicate. It is the highest thing you can do for yourself and for others. Although appearance is a segment of your tool belt, your inner essence is another section. Raising your economic status allows flexibility in the world we live in now, particularly in terms of health and social benefits. Specific application of your femininity and charisma can balance economic equality for all women.

The human brain and body are directly connected to our early concepts of how we fit into the world, what is natural, and the difference between dreams and reality. Our brain lacks ethics or morality, according to the International Brain Education Association (IBREA)[1]. There are pilot programs being conducted around the world by the IBREA, combining different mind/body techniques to help people sustain optimal physical, cognitive, and emotional health levels. These efforts

---

[1] *Brain World,* Issue 2, Vol 3, Winter 2012

are intended to help people connect with the deeper nature inside their brain, or from my perspective, expand and exercise our personal capacity for connectedness.

Deep inside ourselves, we essentially have a desire for peace, harmony, and community. The discord and competitiveness instilled in us as a sense of lack is one of the main causes of violence and our global problems. The work of the IBREA has been tested in some of the most violent places around the world to see if an expanded consciousness and sense of connectedness with the natural environment and fellow humans would have a positive effect.

What is relevant about this and FLIRTonomics? Connecting is a natural thing that humans want and crave. It's as essential to our survival as our external consumption. We increase our likelihood of connection and energetic engagement when we are aware of our natural environment and of others around us. It's often been said we use only 10% of our brain and its capacity. In fact, there are studies on this concept and an institution dedicated to it.

With FLIRT, we awaken emotional connection and empathic states; we ingrain it more deeply into who we are and how we communicate with others. We have different styles. Some people are soft and quiet about their engagements, while others are more overt and boisterous. How you develop your awareness and express it is very specific to you, yet it must be shared to be effective. Studies by the IBREA show that significant positive changes can occur, even in third-world countries where life has lost its value and meaning for many. Peer relationships improved as stress, trauma, and levels of violence were reduced. They call it BE, for brain education, and some recipients of the treatments said they recovered their dreams during sleep. The larger impact of this study takes personal development into the global environment with the objective of peace.

The language used to describe compassionate communication is empathic connection; I call it FLIRTing. This is at the core of what we are striving for in all of our relationships. The external methods for attracting the attention and willingness to engage, and the deeper desire to listen and be present for others starts the process of richer communication and connection.

Our Bond

In *The Bond, Connecting through the Space Between Us,* McTaggart says we operate in this lonely fashion because we see ourselves in an ego-driven way, as separate from everything. That "the thing we call 'I,' is a separate entity, a unique creation of genetic code that lives apart from everything else." Our solitude is a form of mental separation that starts first in our mind and then can be further manifested as we steel ourselves against each other and the world outside of our physical bodies. McTaggart's premise is that this is completely incorrect and that we are all connected. McTaggart is also the author of *The Intention Project.*

Since we rely so heavily on science and the idea of concrete absoluteness that it brings with its time stamping and signatures, it was no small relief to find there are many studies going on all over the world to lend proof to the concept that our separateness is unnecessary and that things are effectively working in conjunction with one another. McTaggart reveals that quantum physics, sociology, and biology all point in the idea that we are far less individual, isolated, or alone than we thought. The focus in American society on independence is not supported by research or natural law. Independence is a masculine concept. Interdependence is a more feminine concept. McTaggart challenges the concept of survival of the fittest with research that reveals adaptations have more to do with social needs than survival needs.

This integrated concept of social interaction and communication are embraced by many of the top leadership writers and teachers, including Franklin Covey, Rudolf Steiner, Hank Fieger, William Drucker and Kate Levinson. In the search for understanding how the brain and internal biochemistry operate, we hope to find out positive clues that will help society operate positively. With technology and these studies, the opportunity for a collaborative conversation is on the forefront. It may solve many social issues. FLIRTonomics speaks to the positive engagement of others in universal language for mutual benefits.

The Human Brain

How we are operating in our day-to-day lives is determined by our thinking and assumptions dictated by our specific experiences and conditions. These ideas both create and are created by a social environment for our interactions with others. In my research over the years, I came to understand and believe that it was not just our minds that govern our actions. Our minds can talk us into or out of anything, given the right circumstances and scenario. Our emotions and our bodies will instruct us otherwise. When we have a gut reaction to something that is the opposite of what we thought we were going to be doing, it is a great time to stop for a moment and take our impulses seriously. Our ability to step away from the singular influence of the mind and integrate other influences causing our reactions enables us to assess from a more holistic approach. We can choose our responses, feelings, and actions.

The Human Mind

Your mind dictates and controls the stories it creates. These stories are extremely powerful and can affect your self-perception in permanent ways, but they can also be redirected. While growing up, I paid little regard to my appearance until I reached puberty and everything came on me like an avalanche. In my experience, I led with my mind or intelligence, and I navigated with my intuition. It's different to be shy than it is to be insecure. When you want or need something, you must confront shyness or go without. Insecurity tells you that you don't deserve it; shyness just holds you back from initiating. Taking steps to ask for what you need and negotiating those terms is one way of working through shyness to get what you want. Flirting or engaging pleasantly makes this much easier. Leveraging your appearance or method of engaging is part of skill development. It creates more security because it compounds with positive results. As a child and young woman, a focus on social fluency and ease of engagement is a good start, particularly when it involves really paying attention to people. Learn to notice what is going on around you as a young age. As child, being pretty was not in any part of my mental framework or experience. I never considered personal beauty and knew I would have to focus on my self-presentation, posture, and intellectual confidence. It is one of the best tools my mother passed on to me because it affects everyone I come in contact with.

We construct stories in our minds to navigate our fears and our environments. We can use these stories or affirmations to support our interdependence and decision making. Old stories can sometimes treat us poorly or entangle our positive progress. We also assess and create stories based on our interactions with others and their stories. Have you ever felt that someone had taken over your story and privately labeled it as their own? I have many times ... at first it was aggravating, then I tried to think of it as flattering, now I realize it is simply a way of relating and it has more to do with them than anything else.

Biology

Fundamentally, we are driven to work in partnerships. How do we know this to be true? If I were a philosopher, it would be a simple exercise in critical thinking. Partnerships and connections are the first things we seek. It is instinctual. Later, our minds, which have been trained to think in terms of lack and fear, question our instincts and we find reason to see separateness. From this perspective, we can assume that we are trained to work against our natural state of cooperation and communication. In my experience, I've found that most communication blocks between relatively normal humans are caused by fear. Once the fear is put to rest or set aside, many wonderful things can begin to occur.

There is a chemical reaction that starts in the body with engagement, attraction, and positive interactions. According to research, the human brain's acquisition of experience of what we see around us is not imaginative. We filter everything through our own experiences, or as I have said, stories we construct based on experience that may or may not be true. We have internal conversations going on all the time with our environments. Highly emphatic people do this at a molecular level via "biophoton emissions," These are small light emissions that emanate from all living organisms, including humans that convey excited states. They prove the connectedness between all organisms and are the focus of a great deal of medical research. In the context of this book, I am simply placing an idea in your mind that we are all more related and can access higher degrees of communication than we may have thought. This premise increases your personal power and influence for the positive.

Connectedness

The human need for connectedness is exhibited on a daily basis. It is something I have come to champion over the past few years, though it is finally being backed up by science. Although quite obvious, humans enjoy and thrive in community and when partnered with others. How we connect and share creates symbiotic relationships, rather than parasitic ones. Manifestation through intention is an illustration of our connectedness and that we can connect with what we need at will. If recent studies can offer a concrete reason for why people are able to manifest and find connection between what they need and what arrives, we are one step closer to the realization that we are a united planet, versus an isolated one. Enhancing our charisma and ability to FLIRT and engage with others will only accelerate this connection process. Not only does it create a foundation for heightened awareness, it also creates a bond between us and those we interact with.

INTERVIEW WITH ALLANA PRATT,
Goddess of Love and Joy, Relationship Expert, Author, Speaker, Coach

Some people are a little racier than others when it comes to considering them for an interview. You never know if their fame will have gone to their heads or into their hearts. Allana Pratt's resides in her heart. She reveals so much of herself to anyone who happens to spend time on her site, it's almost impossible not to fall in love with her gracious, feminine joy. So many snippets pop out I have quickly come to call them Allana-isms.

In our discussion about how we view ourselves and that reflection to the outside, Allana relived her early modeling experiences.

"Good men don't want to be slimes, abuse us, or hold us down. They want to celebrate us. There's nobility in them that wakes up when we own our Queen inside. So when I walk down the runway and feel, 'Yes, I am a work of art. Thanks for noticing,' men straighten up. Be you, be feminine, be authentic, be all of who you are. I don't think we need to shut down half of who we are at work and be someone else at home."

"We are energetic beings, we can't escape that. So when we shrink or we defend, either way, we're either squelching our power or giving away our power. So where's the place that we can be in a sweet spot in our full potency? It comes when we see ourselves as a work of art, something divine and beautiful inside and out."

"It's not easy to get to a place where you know you're a work of art. There's a lot of internal work these women need to do to heal the shame, heal the anger, heal the sadness, heal the betrayal, heal the abandonment, heal whatever issues happen to us as we grew up. But once we do and we are literally madly in love with exactly who we are, we begin treating ourselves with this sense of worship that we are eliciting from the men and women around us. That sense of worship can be simply eating well, sleeping well, or putting cream on your body after the shower."

In our work to overcome old ideas around flirting and it's conversion to energetic engagement, Allana noted how important our intentions are.

"Start from fullness, 'Hey, I can flirt with the breeze and the trees and with you and with guys and with kids, and like I'm just a big flirt with life!'

"If you start to see flirting in that way, you'll be full all the time and you'll never come from that is bad! No, it's not! Lighting up a room when you come in is somehow manipulation. No, it's not! empty place where flirting is manipulation. You really own what it is to be feminine. We judge so many feminine qualities, like being soft is bad. No, it's not! Like smiling It is a gift."

This idea of intention surrounds all of our actions and our thinking about us and others.

"First, recognize how your point of view creates your reality. Not the other way round, and your judgment of another holds their behavior in place. Now you can stop the judging and start the curiosity."

My favorite Allana-ism: *"I don't fix people, but I am the space in which transformation occurs."*

Tactile

People need to be touched. We are developing and maintaining consumer-driven, worker-bee societies that need to discourage touch because it creates bonds and tells more about a person that anything else.

I interviewed someone, who told me about an accident in which another car hit his. The person who hit them stopped their car, jumped out and came running around to talk with him. They were excited, scared, and aggressive. They were shouting and waving their arms around. My friend just reached out, put his hand on the other person's shoulder and said, "It's going to be okay."

"It was like an electric shock went through the guy," he said.

"The guy immediately stopped yelling and flailing his arms. He just stood there and pulled all of that energy back into his body."

"Thank you," the man said. Then he walked over, got out a pen, and wrote down his name and insurance information.

"The thing is, it could have gone completely the other way. I could have joined him in the yelling and arm waving. We might have ended up rolling around fighting a few minutes later if I had not touched him and grounded him back in his body awareness."

As women, there is magic in our touch. We heal and communicate with it. In our communications and in our FLIRTing, touch can mean different things. Appropriate touch and awareness is important, particularly in a society that has distorted its meaning. In American culture, touch has been discouraged over the years for reasons ranging from germs to legal concerns. Because of this, many people are uncomfortable with being touched, so it is important to be aware of individual boundaries and body language.

When you learn to FLIRT, you connect with people on many levels. FLIRTing makes you approachable because it involves smiling, laughter, and engagement. It makes people more comfortable with you and gives them insight in your character.

EXERCISE

Explore your intuition and biological response to interactions with people. Do you feel good, bad, tired, exhausted, or energized from your interactions with them? Do you feel lonely, emotional, or compulsive after spending time with them and observing their behaviors and interactions with others? Are there red flags or white flags flying?

Person	Emotional Response	Energetic Response

CHAPTER 5

Why FLIRT is a Source of Capital

*We're not asking for superiority for we have always had that;
all we ask is equality.*
-Nancy Witcher Langhorne Astor

FLIRT is a source of capital because it opens doors to build wealth in the form of money, as well as in the forms of friendships and culture. FLIRT is a source of capital because it is capital itself and it can be exchanged or used to acquire other forms of capital. You can use it to build a business, a relationship, get investments, and open doors.

Many famous women throughout history leveraged their personal capital, femininity, and charisma to support causes, build empires, and create social change. You can build your wealth on FLIRT, using intelligence and cultural skills to support it.

USE YOUR PERSONAL CAPITAL AS A SOURCE OF OTHER TYPES OF CAPITAL

"I like to do business with people I like, that I want to spend time with. I want to work with people who care about the world, who are honest, hardworking, and do a good job. I'm very selective. I like people who have a lot of energy and who are going to be fun to be around."
~ Jessica Scorpio, Founder and Director of Marketing for Getaround.com

Overcoming Gender Stereotypes and Stigmas

The gender stereotypes of femininity have influenced aggression toward women when they break from social ideals, despite them being stereotypical and not based in reality. The stereotypes often portray women as having more manual dexterity and sensitivity than men and being more attractive. These stereotypes have allowed women to be placed into segregated occupational roles. These restricted roles are contrived to fill needed job descriptions by women, while leaving others free for men. In 1942, when the war ended and the men returned from overseas, women were encouraged to step aside and move back into the occupational roles designed specifically for their gender to allow men to re-enter the workforce.

The focus on the feminine is a response to many women who feel they must give up their femininity to compete in the same economic environment as men, as if they are men. Appreciation of our femininity, our bodies, and our sensuality actually opens doors we did not even know were closed. In many ways, our society has worked to suppress the feminine charisma of women and girls. It is time to stop asking women to work with the handicap of a professional athlete. It has been giving the male population an unfair economic benefit and society a sense of discontent because things don't quite match up. People are forced to decide between marriage, children, or work. Women prefer work/life balance because their real workload is so heavy.

Women in the workforce have an ever-growing powerful position, yet they still lag economically. According to *Harvard Business Review* in 2011, men start their careers in higher paying positions than women post MBA. These "first jobs set the stage for all the inequities that follow" women throughout their careers. Women are only earning $.80 cents for every dollar earned by a man. While this shows improvement over the last 30 years, it's not what you would expect, considering the education level and job variety. Motherhood and parenting appear to have become unattractive, as well, with 63% of female managers remaining childless, versus 57% of male managers. Motherhood takes a greater toll on a women's paycheck, and much of this can go unnoticed, even in a married family with dual incomes. This may point to the decrease in marriage and child-rearing in the U.S. and many European countries.

Statistically, women represent fewer than 15% of the corporate executive positions in top companies worldwide and just 3% of CEO positions in Fortune 500 Companies. There are many reasons to be considered, from the fact that most of these companies are run by the male population, to biological reasons like childbearing, and roles that defer to women per social norms. Still, even without the childbearing aspect, women remain at a 20% deficit or more.

Now consider your femininity and charisma as a source of capital. The 50 top female earners in the U.S. and internationally are noted for their femininity and charisma. As a source of capital, your personal assets can be leveraged and accessed at any age and in any situation. They must be applied to building social, cultural. and economic capital together to reach your desired outcome.

INTERVIEW WITH JESSICA SCORPIO,
Founder and Director of Marketing for Getaround.com

I asked Jessica if I could interview her because she is a successful, young, entrepreneurial woman under 30 years old. I wanted to hear firsthand if she used FLIRT in her business and how she feels about women leveraging their assets professionally.

"Women definitely should leverage all their assets in business. Young women are not dressing how they want. Professional clothing can be form fitting to the female body. Women have so many assets in terms of tangible skills and set a nice balanced tone to the team or office. It is really important to have as many women in the company as possible. There are more and more female founders, business leaders, leaders of non-profits. I see that starting to happen. Women should be less concerned about what people think than they are.

Women help create a more fun and positive environment with their female energy. It's important to aware of and respect boundaries. I go above and beyond to make it clear I am about business, but I treat men and women the same."

Are there challenges for women in business?

"Yes, there are so many challenges to being a woman. Women have to be tougher and harder working than guys. I also think there are a lot of benefits. My co-founders recognize that there are a lot of things I bring to the table. They rely on my creativity, perspective, and intuition. Those are skills and strengths that women bring to the table, but sometimes I wonder, "Why is it so hard!"

Do you FLIRT in business?

"People often ask me why I am so good at networking. What I tell them is that I am good at connecting with people. I listen to what they have to say and what they are about. I can assess them very quickly, and then I remember them and what we talked about. Being a little flirty can help gain access to them."

How do you leverage your charisma as the face of the brand, Getaround?

"People like to use products from companies where they know someone. So for Getaround, I go out to events, I am on line telling our story. We try and do video, social media, photos, rich content that can display your charisma. So charisma can be created via marketing and public venues. Charisma is about being passionate and conveying that passion for your product or cause. In general, people want to work with people who are passionate. I am very passionate about helping people improve their lives. I definitely communicate that passion. I do not think there is much difference between how I communicate with men or women, but I am definitely very passionate and communicate my charisma that way."

Is charisma teachable?

"Charisma can be learned and honed. There are a lot of really great coaches for leadership and public speaking. I recommend people use coaches to help them get better at certain things—finding your spark and what you are passionate about and then communicating that passion and honing it. Charisma is about conveying your passion, positive energy, and enthusiasm."

Do you have any advice for women using FLIRT to network?

"Openness is a key aspect of the connection. One of the things I tell people when they are looking to connect with people is don't be laser focused on how to work a room [how you can get what you want] really fast. Try to be open and connect with people by having fun. If you are having fun, you will be better at networking, telling people your story, and getting people to support you."

Getaround is a marketplace for car sharing. Getaround enables car owners to car share when they are not using it, and for people to gain access to cars when they need one. Owners earn about $300/month, and renters can get access to cars from Roadsters to a Prius.

Getaround is currently in San Francisco CA, San Diego CA, Austen TX and Portland OR. Our car owners are provided with up to $1,000,000 of coverage, plus roadside assistance and 24-hour support. Getaround has raised about $3.4 million in capital, not including the Series A funding which will be public soon.

Our Heroines and FLIRT

When we look at our feminine heroines over the years, they come in the form of mythology, archetypes, historical figures, and leaders, as well as comic book versions of modern-name myths, like Wonder Woman or some of the more obscure ones we can find in comic strips today. Female heroines are meant to empower women and girls, but also to entertain men who read more comics than women. The female figures of mythology exhibit many of the qualities of holistic feminine, charisma, and eroticism. They also exhibit power, strength, and determination—attributes often associated with men. These are human attributes applied in a feminine way. Female heroines are independent, sexy (feminine curves), direct, and tender at the same time. In mythology, they can also be quite brutal, from Durga to Athena.

Cleopatra- Ultimate Muse using FLIRT

Cleopatra is known for her exquisite manipulation of men and power through her intelligence and beauty. She was left in a position of joint power with her young brother and was forced by social law to marry him to maintain family power, but she soon revealed she had no intention of sharing the throne. She was highly intelligent and skilled in the areas of politics, strategy, seduction, charm, charisma, fitness, self-presentation, fertility, nurture, and vitality. She had a fabulous sense of humor and was creative, as demonstrated in her games and bets with her two husbands and in her antics to gain support for politics and power. She used her femininity to secure interdependence and maintain her position of power for her country. She was noted for her communication skills, both in the languages she spoke and in her delivery through performance and tone. Communication is a skill that is learned from early childhood on and then applied to situations and circumstances. Your willingness to learn and apply communication through voice, actions, mannerisms, and energy is measured by your desire for an outcome. Cleopatra understood the power of seduction and allure and the importance of thinking at full capacity. She was wife, warrior, and mother. She wasted no time on loose ends and made sure her relationships with her supporters was complete, without distractions or disaffections. She understood the power of self-presentation, health, and vitality. Vitality comes from humor, engagement, flirting, and eating well. She was known for her dinner parties, humorous behavior, and most certainly her fertility, both of the body and of the mind. She embodied a whole and healthy charismatic woman.

In many snippets of writing about Cleopatra, people throw in her large nose or that she was a seductress rather than a genius. I found these little digs to be humorous but see them as an attempt to limit her beauty or discount her power. Mentions like these exemplify how society tries to limit the perception of beauty to a specific ideal and discourage women from assuming all aspects of femininity, relegating importance to one aspect of the whole. The female ideal is one of mother, lover, warrior, ruler, diplomat, creative, strategist, appreciator of beauty, and being well versed in the skill of nurture. Had Cleopatra not had a balance of attributes and the intelligence to develop and enhance them, she may not been as affluent, memorable, or successful.

Cleopatra used the breadth of her femininity, charisma, and intelligence not only to capture the attention of Anthony and Caesar, but also to garner agreements from her armies and her people. Women do this in their daily lives as they navigate the care of their children or politics of the workplace. Yet, they do it with a handicap. We can all be modern Cleopatras, leveraging our intelligence, wit, and sensuality to balance power and support passions and joy in various aspects of our lives. While she was in a different time and needed to manage a position of power, so, too, do women today in order to balance the economic deficit. One can only imagine what would happen if women implemented these skills with some degree of attention, sidestepping social labeling and male-inspired handicaps.

Cleopatra used personal capital to gain land, property, culture, followers, supporters, and economic gain. All capital can be exchanged for another. It is a simple matter of filling the right need at the right time. When we need to cut grain in the field, we need a machine or human capital to do the job. Whether we need a leader who is charismatic and balanced or someone who can get in and get the job done, we may be looking for you.

All women of power possess charisma and used it to create to leverage their causes and sometimes economic status. The most noted used it to align and build community around policy changes for women and minorities. From Eleanor of Aquitaine, to Hatshepsut, Joan of Arc, Catherine de Medici, Elizabeth I, Jane Addams, Nancy Witcher-Langhorne Astor, Clara Barton, Ella Baker, Eleanor Roosevelt, Margaret Sanger, Gloria Steinem, Harriet Tubman, Mary Wollstonecraft and many others,[2] we find women who used their social grace, charisma, and femininity to garner support for their causes. Many of them found powerful life partners; others found collaborators who supported their causes.

Gloria Steinem is known as the mother of feminism, although feminism had been going on for a couple hundred years before she came on the scene. Interestingly, Steinem used her beauty and intelligence to expose sexism and

---

[2] Names taken from http://www.angelfire.com/anime2/100import/

harassment. She leveraged her assets for political voice. She has since been a powerful influence on policy change, using her femininity, sexuality, charisma, and intelligence to open doors and cement relationships, resulting in powerful political change.

Women were advocating the same women's issues in the 1800's we face today. Margaret Sanger was one such woman who publically published and talked about the issues of unwanted and repeated pregnancies against the 1873 Comstock law, arguing for birth control. She began a daily news column about sex called *What Every Girl Should Know*, as well as *The Woman Rebel*, which was banned. She was indicted for obscenity but jumped bail and went to England under an alias, where she released 100,000 copies of a pamphlet about the use of contraceptives called *Family Limitation*. Sanger did not stop her fight for contraception; despite being jailed and harassed, she went in the face of conflict for what was right. To be able to institute and create change, you must have a unique ability to get support and lead. This is FLIRT, charisma, femininity, and persuasion. It is not sexual. That is a distraction attempting to discourage women from using their most important and powerful tools.

Jane Addams wrote many books on prostitution, women's rights, juvenile delinquency, and military force. She was charismatic and powerful in politics... much is left unsaid here about her femininity, but her writings reveal the topics of importance in her fight for economic equality for women and children. Clara Barton worked with Susan B Anthony in women's suffrage and raised enough funds to enable her to move more comfortably in her support of many of her efforts against slavery and women's economic issues. She created the Red Cross in the United States.

At Eve Ensler's lecture in 2012, she said, "We don't know joy in this country." She had a point. Completely unfettered joy that has no boundaries is an amazing feeling and pure in its requirements. We stifle it here. Ensler was discussing the miracle of City of Joy, where women and girls go to heal. They relearn joy and to love their bodies. Smiling and the expression of joy should be a practice of expression, not a burden. Many women seem to have had a complete disconnect between the expression of joy and its reciprocal benefits, turning to short-term fixes like Prozac and other pills as a solution. Smiling is an exercise that has become difficult, despite it being an answer to the problem. Your sense of health and well-being encourages others to engage with you and gives you the energy you need. With our inhibited behaviors and social judgments, we find ourselves looking around, wondering why we are not as happy as it seems we should be. We walk with tension and resistance to that which is actually buried within us. Instead of barring others from entering our scope, perhaps we are barring ourselves from breaking out of our patterns.

Changing our thinking about using our personal assets to get what we want will not only make us more successful and more efficient, it will make us happier, freeing blocked areas within ourselves. Women set the barometer in many social and work environments. Our self-talk, attitudes, and FLIRT are something we can change ourselves.

EXERCISE

Take this little sample test. The rest of it can be found on my website at www.flirtonomics.net. Think about your answers and how a shift might make you more efficient, professionally and personally.

Rate each question on a scale of 1-5,
1 being the lowest, 5 being the highest.

		Not Satisfied/ Satisfied/Very Satisfied				
Humor		1	2	3	4	5
1.	Do you laugh often?					
2.	Do you laugh more at work or at home?					
3.	Do you practice joking around?					
4.	Are you offended easily?					
5.	Do you forgive easily?					
Social Grace						
1.	Are you comfortable entering a crowded room?					
2.	Do you enjoy making introductions?					
3.	Do you smile easily at strangers?					
4.	Do you know body language?					
5.	Do you pay attention to others well?					

Total Score: _____

10-20 pts: You have some serious happiness ahead of you.

20-35 pts: You need to take a take a look and see where disconnects are. Happiness is coming.

35-45 pts: Test some small adjustments and have fun seeing how a slight change can make a mega difference.

50 pts, Congrats! You can put these two aside and focus on one of the other areas!

CHAPTER 6

How to Get Your FLIRT On!

Cultivate your curves—they may be dangerous,
but they won't be avoided.
~Mae West

People who flirt or engage their charisma are using their personal tool chest to build relationships quickly. In order to upset the competitive advantage relationship building creates, people may label all flirting as sexual and inappropriate. Just remember, it is a competitive move. Flirting is a positive and doesn't hurt anyone when done in the right way at the right time.

"People often ask me why I am so good at networking. What I tell people is that I am good at connecting with people, I listen to what they have to say and what they are about. I can assess them very quickly and then I remember them and what we talked about. Being a little flirty can help gain access to them."
~Jessica Scorpio, Founder Getaround

FLIRT starts with smiling. Sorry, it just does! Humans need to be smiled at to get confirmation of whether they are dealing with a friend or foe. Being friendly is about demonstrating to someone else in a common language that you are not going to cause them harm. Smiling, open palms, body language, head angle, and facial expression are fairly universal. Some cultures may have tighter or looser guidelines around who it is appropriate to approach or when it is, but body language is fairly common across cultures.

"I absolutely use flirting in business. It is a level of openness. Unmarried women are more receptive and open because they think they cannot have male relationships. This does not benefit us as women because we shut off that side of ourselves that is playful. Operating from a level of openness can be done without gender differentiation." Mira Veda, Founder Lipstick & Politics

Social charm is how you grease the wheels of social engagement with anyone. Having a strong sense of cultural behavior and what is expected in situations will make your life easier and put people at ease. Familiarity brings repeat customers. They know what to expect and can enjoy their experience and interaction with you more fully. Since this book is called *FLIRTonomics, How to Capitalize on Your Femininity and Charisma without Sleeping with Anyone*, addressing the illusive aspect of how to define femininity would be useful. Generally speaking, I am a playful flirt. I have no exclusions. I will flirt with babies, girls, boys, men, women, co-workers, and people I've never met in my life—just about anyone who will engage I will try to get to smile.

FLIRTING IS LEARNED

Flirting is a learned behavior, and it can be developed into your personal behavior repertoire. As a steadfast introvert passionate about nature, animals, and children, I had little interest or skills in social playground politics. I was advanced in my young assessment of my family's economic situation. Our lack of economic capital shaped the way we approached things and our emotional currency around money. I knew I would have to negotiate for what I wanted when it came to anything that involved money. My parents did not have an extra dollar to spend on any of my animal-raising tactics or pen obsessions. I knew I would need to use communication skills to get by and to be able to ask for what I wanted. I read about posture, poise, and communication skills in books like *The Five Little Peppers*, the book series by Margaret Sidney. The children were poor, but creative, inspired, and happy working together. They embodied some aspect of my lifestyle growing up and my ideals around what makes people happy.

I found ways around my introversion, using mannerisms and tactics I had read about and tried. It was the most difficult challenge of my life, and residuals of my introversion still remain. But introverts turned extroverts usually do not change completely. There are ways to get what you need without asking directly, including bartering. I began negotiating the price of renting horse pastures for my ponies when I was about 10 years old. I also bought, traded, and rescued horses and became known as the one to call when a wild bird was found alongside the road or the horses were running through town. My inner vitality, intention, nurturing skills, and creativity were well formed, even as my social skills were not. I earned a reputation and a persona of trust. This is the first step of fledgling charisma.

An early entrepreneur, I discovered I could make money by selling things. I created a stuffed animal called an "Emmu," which I made of rabbits fur I sewed myself. I sold them at school for $3 to $7, depending on the size. Let's just say that this small fad was lucrative since I acquired the skins for under $3 and could make 3 to 5 Emmus from it. If I had not been using some of the skills in FLIRTonomics, I probably would not have been able to sell anything. Somehow, I made the creations limited, alluring, exclusive, and cool. I did this with the intention of leveraging the mysterious and exclusive nature of a handmade item, but if I had been socially skilled and had the power of FLIRT, I'm sure I would have benefited even more from the endeavor.

HOW TO GET YOUR FLIRT ON:

Be Friendly (engage), show Leadership through initiative and relaxed confidence, be Inquisitive and interested in others, be Receptive to their response, make contact with Tactile communication. Above all, FLIRTing is fun. If you are not having fun, you are doing it wrong. Perhaps you are not doing it in a way that is comfortable to you. There are different types of flirting and ways we can leverage our assets to open connection. You have to use the one that is right for you.

TYPES OF FLIRTING

Flirting can be used to communicate to another person the prospect of physical intimacy. It's the most titillating definition of the word that's the one that people tend to think of because, in definition, it means to attract, yet often with a lack of seriousness (in romantic attention). Flirting is very light, whereas seduction is a much more direct and purposeful word. It is specifically defined by the intent to connect in an intimate way. We are not primarily interested in seductive flirting for the sake of FLIRTonomics, but human nature will remain human nature. We are looking at FLIRT for energetic engagement to be directed at will.

There are at least five types of flirting. There's playful flirting, traditional flirting, polite flirting, and sincere flirting. Flirting involves body language, tone of voice, laughter, engagement, and eye contact.

Which type of FLIRT are you?

Physical

Physical flirts convey their connection and attraction through body language and emotional expression. Eye contact, touching, hair flipping or playfulness, and proximity to the counterpart are physical expressions of flirting. Verbal wordplay and clever entendres are threaded into off topic areas in fun and jest.

Traditional

Traditional flirts often misunderstand non-flirting as flirting. They are blocked by the old idea that flirting is bad and only sexual in meaning. As a result, they have a tendency to hold back and miss out on social fun. Word play and light banter fall into the traditional category.

Polite

Polite flirting is manner-driven and non-sexual. Polite flirts are constrained and very aware of how their flirting is being interpreted. They have a tendency to judge flirtatious behavior and how and when it is appropriate. Small talk, smiling, and light teasing is polite flirting. Jests are never sexual or political in nature.

Sincere

Sincere flirts are confident, willing to express emotion, and respond to chemistry. Sincere flirts use open smiles and a respectful distance with their intent at the forefront of the engagement.

Playful

Playful flirt do so for fun. They use no age, gender, or social distinctions between people they will engage with. They flirt often and casually as a form of communication. They are open and use flirting to enhance self-esteem and build connection. They use flirting to makes others feel important and positive.

Flirting has no gender bias. Men and women flirt to smooth out social situations, as well as indicate interest or just have fun. Knowing the type of flirt you are makes it easier to see which situations work best for you and where you can venture into other areas to leverage up your level of engagement. Understanding the types of flirting can also help you understand what might make someone else uncomfortable. The purpose of FLIRT is to create positive interactions and more intimate relationships.

APPROPRIATE VS. INAPPROPRIATE FLIRTING

Appropriate	Reaction	Inappropriate	Reaction
Smiling	Smiling in return	Leering	Cringing in return
Joking	Laughing in response	Joking, crudely	Eyes break away and body language retracts
Patting on the arms	Pat in return	Patting on the arm	Moving body into protective stance
Eye contact in smiling	Eyes smile in return	Eye contact too long	Fidgeting and eyes break away
Friendly conversation	Person stays and asks questions to continue	Friendly conversation, off topic	Person moves away and excuses self

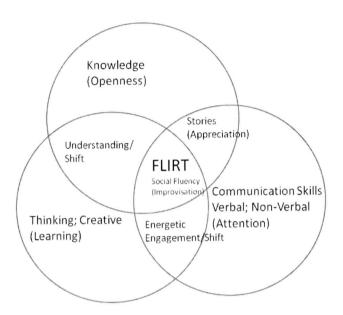

GETTING YOURSELF READY TO FLIRT

Feeling good is a great way to start FLIRTing. Paying some attention to your personal style and presentation will give you confidence and make you more receptive to engaging with others. On one hand, you must be open to engagement, drawing people to you, but you must also be assertive in extending yourself to others.

Beauty & Presentation

You will feel more beautiful and attractive if you treat yourself like you are beautiful. Clean your skin and enhance your features with make-up, moisturizers, and hair removal. Tweeze your brows or chin; check for blemishes and dry patches. Put yourself together in the appropriate way before you leave the house. It is better to be a bit overdressed than completely underdressed. When you meet people, you will react to them differently if you feel you are in your best presentation. They will also react to you differently because knowing you care about yourself makes them inclined to care about you, as well. This is called perception of value.

It is the same as with anything. Imagine a bit of crockery that you have been told came from your great-great-grandmother. It has been passed down with love through your family. You will treat it as a treasure, even if to someone else, it looks like a broken old dish. When you weave a story around it, it develops symbolic capital. Always carry yourself with your own perception of value. The most successful self-presentation style reflects your true values and respects the conditions of those you are communicating with. You do not need to be a magazine-style beauty to create an impression of beauty and elegance. Your attention to detail and your body language and personal style will convey that message.

Get your FLIRT on by taking care with the image you present and opening an immediate dialogue that resonates with who you are. A smile can override the best suits in the world, but the exterior compounds and confirms the counterpart's belief.

Vitality

Vitality is also a gift you bring with you and share. It is pure unadulterated energy overflow. It can make the most mundane chore a fun adventure. It is all in how you perceive things and choose to explore your experiences. Liveliness makes it a pleasure to share your company. It imbues passion and does not always mean happiness. It can be expressed in passion and emotion. It is present and real.

FLIRTing involves engaging with your inner vitality and exposing it to others. Create inner vitality through your consumptions and through deep breaths that feed your body oxygen. Gather up positive and optimistic thoughts about your day and the people you might encounter. Good humor is a significant part of your vitality, and it ties directly into your diet/consumption, physical fitness, and sense of gratitude.

Gratitude brings things into alignment and often erupts in joyfulness and goodwill. Michio Kushi talks about this and what he learned through his studies with George Ohsawa in his writings on food and mindfulness. Two key elements to a healthy human are vitality, as in enough energy to sustain you daily, and good humor, the ability to transition through small disturbances often.

You share your vital force with others when you engage with them and create an energetic exchange. This energy creates more energy as it connects. This can be felt in a rush of emotion caused by positive or negative engagement. FLIRT focuses on the positive, sharing your inner vitality with a smile, a helping hand, and with a sense of humor.

Get your flirt on by eating well, getting exercise, and looking at life with humor. Even the worst situations can have a sense of irony and humor.

Let go by breathing and allowing laughter to fill you up. Use your vitality to attract people to you.

Metta

Loving kindness. This is an amazing practice defined by operating with love and attention in all levels. It is a great way to get your FLIRT on! This has opened up a lot of love in my life. You can start with something as simple as saying a kind word to the cashier at the grocery store, a person walking through the mall, or by affectionately teasing your child.

Learn to Read Others

If you want to communicate effectively, learn to read others and make them feel comfortable. You can do this through eye contact and by shifting your own body posture. If they appear to be overwhelmed, pull your energy back. If they appear threatened, try putting both hands on the table—for example, where they can see them to show that they are empty.

Psychologically, it's strange, but it can have an immediate effect. As previously mentioned, there are no neutral body moves, so using your body language can attract or repel. Both charisma and FLIRT involve body language.

EXERCISE

Go out with the intention of meeting someone, anyone. Dress up for the occasion so your appearance invites comment. Use open body postures. Note when you engage with someone how long the interaction is, the other person's body language, and how the conversation transitions to ending. Consider your responsibility in the interaction.

Interactions	Body Language Attributes	Conversation Transition

CHAPTER 7

From FLIRTation to Negotiation

If you have knowledge, let others light their candles in it.
~Margaret Fuller

LEVERAGING FLIRTONOMICS

When you FLIRT, you create and build rapport. You also build influence and fall into leadership roles as a result. More than ever before, leadership relies on influence. As a woman, you have the ability to build community, as well as partnerships, very effectively. Using your assets to create and build influence is also very important with regard to building trust and consistency.

Capitalize on Femininity and Charisma

Women can regain personal power by embracing femininity and reclaiming tools that some projects of the feminist movement stripped away from them. Women possess more power and influence than they have been encouraged to use. In the same jobs, they acquire less economic return than men. There are many discussions and theories as to why this is. Some assume it is because men still hold the top positions in the largest highest-paying jobs; others say it is because women do not ask for raises or because women start at a lower pay scale and never catch up. These may all be true, but it could also be that women have not leveraged their feminine power as much as they could or should. It's a tricky business with all the negative labels flying around and men controlling public policy and law. Still, women who are aware of the differences between men and women in work and in play can tip the scale in a way that creates great partnerships. Women seem to have little interest in taking over the world; they want to make it a better place and do it together. As such, they must not buy into the male or Darwinian behaviors that create win/lose scenarios while they navigate the space to create economic equality and better health.

From Social Handicap to Social Currency

An assumption has been implemented by patriarchal rule that women are supposed to give their gifts for free, whereas men get paid for any and all the work they do. When women do it, it is assumed she will do it without pay or acknowledgement. It's taken for granted. This is accepted in addition to the full-time work schedule women are expected to keep in a society that functions most profitably with dual incomes. Yet women hold the "handicap" of more work, lower pay, and not being supported in using their feminine assets to get economic equality. Further, women are expected to volunteer their time (without pay) for schools, foundations, social event planning, etc., as part of their "duty." Since there is no economic exchange for this work, the exchange must be in social capital. Social capital has value, and the skills needed to acquire it are social fluency. This is a currency you can use.

If you think beautiful people get everything for free, just remember, nothing is free and it never has been. There's always a negotiation occurring. Young women are willing to lay their personal currency of youth, beauty, and energy on the table in exchange for economic currency. This is nothing new. Men have been willing to lay out economic or social currency in exchange for feminine company and erotic capital. Men will leverage their economic capital and their social network to acquire fertility when they have a child with a younger woman.

It is all a form of emotional and social currency when it comes to exchanges. Sometimes it involves less tangible trade items; sometimes it involves hard assets.

But how do we turn FLIRT, Friendly, Lively, Inquisitive, Receptive, and Tactile engagements, into a negotiation? You have attracted them, and they have arrived with energy. Now that you have the "floor," it's time to turn the focus on what you are selling. Are you looking for new friendships, networks, jobs, clients, contracts, or investors? Keeping the interest pleasant, not too personal, and leaving enough on the table to inspire another meeting is the object of the interaction. Relationships may open quickly, but they build over time.

Dispel Past Beliefs
"Beautiful women always get what they want."
Studies show that beautiful people may get treated better than those wearing a "fat suit." Those studies have to be revealed for what they are—a person wearing a disguise. Humans sense when someone is disingenuous. They may not be able to tell exactly what the incongruence is, but their instinctual reaction is to get away from anything that is dishonest or appears sick. People wearing fat suits will likely be treated worse than people who are overweight because they are in disguise.

People who are otherwise healthy, energetic, and kind, like Oprah Winfrey, Adele, Mia Amber Davis, Carrie Baker Reynolds, Delta Burke, or Mae West, are weight irrelevant and use charisma for negotiation. They are beautiful and attractive because of whom they are and the actions they take. Sometimes people, beautiful or not, can manage to not ask or demand things directly, but they must convey and communicate what they want or they are unlikely to get it. There are certainly some avenues that are easier for beautiful, healthy people, and others that make things more challenging. The bottom line is that it is up to you to leverage the assets you have and care for yourself in the best way possible.

Learning to receive well and demonstrate appreciation are steps toward acquiring what you need. They are also the key to turning all engagements into excess capital.

INTERVIEW WITH MIRA VEDA,
CEO/Founder of LipstickandPolitics.com

Mira is also co-founder of a technology company called proximityware.

Lipstick & Politics grew out of the necessity to connect with other women and build a community with substance. Misogyny in the media and all the negative projections of women constantly bothered Mira. How do women counter this conversation? How do women who see this meet together and have a forum? It started as a group, then needed a voice on line, so they went beyond her blog and other women started becoming part of the conversation.

Mira is redefining feminism in this generation. Feminists today love sex and men. I wanted to interview Mira because her vision is a powerful voice for the future of women and women in business.

Do you use FLIRT in business?

"Yes, absolutely. It is a level of openness. Unmarried women are more receptive and open [to FLIRT with a woman] because they think they cannot have male relationships. This does not benefit us as women because we shut off that side of ourselves that is playful.

Mira operates with a level of openness and without gender differentiation. It seems relevant and exciting to see women in business working from a position of human behavior versus gender behavior.

Her philosophy:

"Trust the universe and do not be afraid of being hurt by the person you are engaging with or being judged by others. Women behave the way they do because we do not want to be judged by other women or our community. This is a cultural difference. We train [women] to be closed off. Women tend to jump on this process of being critical of each other. This stems from our own insecurities about our place and being in competition with each other over the silliest things. I think it comes down to culture, how we learn to share or do things.

"Like attracts like. If you feel there are not any good men or women, then maybe you should look at how you are operating and how you are behaving. Who are you at this moment in time? Maybe you have not even thought about who you are. It starts with you.

"To be frank, I use the same [process to connect] every time. I am probably more flirtatious with women than with men. With men, there is a fine line, so there is a level of openness, but also a level of discretion. Just so there is enough of a friendship building but not a sexual invitation. I will rein people back if they say something inappropriate and mention they said something 'stupid' just so they have understanding of boundaries.

"I treat both men and women exactly the same. The way I see it, spirit has no gender, so I actually am just as open with men and women. I try not to restrict myself unless I feel like the conversation is heading in a direction that I am uncomfortable with. I use charisma as a tool, a way to really get to know the person who I am talking to. Usually people loosen up when they feel comfortable with someone. For me, charisma has to have that quality, comfort, and desire to want to connect.

Charisma is learned and can be honed. As children, we learn how to smile brighter or flirt to engage others. Somewhere along the way, society or our families knock that behavior out of us. We are asked to act like everyone else. Not get more than our share of attention.

Have you experienced any difficulties as a woman?

"Yes because of the way I look and the way I am. People do not take me as seriously unless I change my tone or act more aggressive. People have a tendency to want to move the conversation to a more personal level. Men always take it back to their primal state. They want to have everything in sight. If they see it, they want it, so there is always some unwanted male attention. Just because you have embraced yourself does not mean it's an invitation for him to embrace [you], as well. Just because you are wearing a pretty dress or red lipstick does not mean you are doing it for anyone but yourself.

What types of people do you like to do business with?

"People I like. Period!

"Obviously, our culture wants to contain women to behave in ways that benefit society, but not necessarily women. I think women have to be the ones to say what fits for them; they are the ones who need to speak up.

"Women should be able to use whatever tools they need to achieve the goals they want. Men use whatever tools necessary to rise to the top, so women shouldn't be afraid to do what they need to do while still acting in a dignified and honorable way. We are social creatures. We should care enough, but not to the point where it alters who we are or what we want to achieve."

For more information about Mira and Lipstick & Politics, go to lipstickandpolitics.com.

One of the most important factors to manage in attraction and business is the clarity of your communications. If you feel misplaced attraction and are concerned about it getting in the way of business relations, address it through compassionate conversation. Stay on task and be appropriate. Intimacy lines can be crossed easily in situations involving talk that is too personal, touching that moves outside of the shoulder/wrist range, and time spent outside of work hours. Respect for each other and the connected people in your lives is more important than energetic impulses. There is a big difference between seduction, manipulation, and friendly flirting. Under no circumstances let the level of your work go down as a result of interactions between yourself and others. Keeping fun and energetic connections in professional environments can make work more pleasurable, create better results, and inspire passion for the product or task at hand.

Men ask for what they want. Women do not do it as often or ask for as much as men. Sometimes it seems like men actually understand the value of feminine capital better than women. Men are willing to do all sorts of things for female company and attention. Nonetheless, it is important to know what you want when you are negotiating with men or women. While FLIRT can be used to open doors regardless of gender or age, you still need to ask for what you want. Don't negotiate yourself down in your head before you start.

Negotiation Skills

1. Negotiations are always done with a Win-Win attitude. If they weren't, they would not be negotiations; they would be theft or invasion. Negotiations are for long-term relationships. Always assume your relationships will be long-term.
2. Communicate with your counterpart or partner.
3. Be fair and be trustworthy.
4. You have already used your charisma and social fluency to develop rapport and trust.
5. Negotiations are a positive way of structuring your communication process with your counterpart.

6. Remember the extra level of value you are bringing to the table with your personal assets. It's not all cut and dried anymore.

7. Consider the long-term effects of your engagement and relationship building. Your counterpart certainly is.

Getting what you want takes leadership and negotiation skills. It takes communicating in the right way to the right people. Your tools are your power of attraction and your different languages.

Negotiations Can Come Up Any Time

A woman once told me a story about a relationship she was in that was not economically equal. The man wanted to buy a house with her because their credit and income together would make it possible. He agreed to pay more of the mortgage because he made more money and he would use one of the four bedrooms for his office. Two of the rooms were to be used by her children, and there was no space for her to call her own. About a month after the purchase of the home, he told her he felt it was unfair that she paid less and her children used more space. He wanted her to pay more of the mortgage. Although she did not make enough to sustain the payment for long, she thought for a moment and agreed to pay half. Her job paid a fixed salary, and there was no way to increase her income, as it was not a sales or commission job, but in her mind she had quickly calculated she might be able to get another job and enroll in graduate school.

Fourteen days later, she was sitting in a classroom, enrolled in graduate school with a student loan to back her. The man was not happy. He wanted her to either get dependant by marrying him, which would justify in his mind the differentiated financial obligations, or get independent. When she enrolled in school and would still not marry him, he felt threatened and treated it like it was just another potential financial and time burden without the commitment.

When she got a job a couple of months later in sales and doubled her salary for the second time in two years, he was even more anxious. He felt insecure and did not like the social side of the sales cycle, which always involves flirting. He knew this aspect as a salesman himself. All he saw was trouble, yet he still wanted her to pay more, but with one hand tied behind her back. It had been no small feat to get into graduate school in a matter of days with applications and interviews, and be admitted in such a short time. She was serious, passionate, and told her story at her interview to get in. She engaged and allured with her history and background, using charisma to get things to move just a little more quickly than usual. That was an economic use of her time and her thinking, and she was fully committed to the outcome.

As a result, the relationship with the man broke off because he could not stop the jealousy and harassment while she tried to focus on school. In the USA, she did what she is able to do here. She moved out and continued with her program. In other countries and even other places or relationships, this may not have been possible. Other women may have succumbed to the bullying and dropped out of school under the pressure.

Exercise of Intention

Our intention is more transparent that we want to believe. When we do things with intention, our internal body chemistry changes and it is evident in the way others respond to us. How we feel about what we are doing changes our body language, our tone, and our eye contact. Intention is not control; it is direction facing toward a positive outcome. When we face or assume a negative outcome, we are likely to create that response, as well.

As a woman, I've noticed we often worry about what others will think about our intention or how it will be perceived by people other than the one we are addressing. When your intention is clear and focused on the best outcome, then it is clear to the person you are communicating with and matters little what sideline translators think.

EXERCISE

Make a practice of clearing your mind before each encounter or situation you may be entering into. If you are experiencing fear or anxiety about an event, a meeting, or a conversation, focus on what your intention is and three possible outcomes. These outcomes should be most desired and an acceptable reaction for a lesser desired outcome. In this way, you can focus in and consider how the best desired outcome also benefits the person or situation you will be engaging with. Try this before any meeting.

If you have anxieties, try creating a mantra with a positive outcome to say 10 times before the meeting. Write them down to make them clear:

1. _____
2. _____
3. _____
4. _____
5. _____

CHAPTER 8

Situational Application of FLIRTonomics

Laughter is good for thinking because when people laugh,
it is easier for them to admit new ideas to their minds.
~His Holiness Tenzin Gyatso, the 14th Dalai Lama

What's Really Moving the Economy

Goods and services—tangible and intangible—are moving the economy. Their exchange, acquisition, and people's passions move our communities. We buy, sell, trade, and barter our time and money to feed our families and create life's experiences. Leadership is essential when it comes to creating and affecting change in our society. But do not mistake the power of sexuality harnessed by Charisma and Social Intelligence.

Taking Action

As women, we need to learn and develop the tools we are given and stock up on the aspects that will fade over time. We must share them with each other and teach them to our children, male and female, so that they can move with success and confidence through society in personal and professional engagements. It's all about communication and being very good at it. It's about understanding what is going on in your own body and recognizing what is happening with other people. It is about increased awareness and noticing the reactions we evoke and the ones going on inside us and others that tell us about their physical, mental, and emotional health. We can become our own physicians and perform our own set of diagnostics on those we encounter. The fact is we do it already without even realizing it. I am only suggesting we become more aware of it and use our language, our words, and our presence to communicate at the highest levels we are capable of with integrity and depth. I am also very much suggesting that we use these more developed qualities in ourselves to build economic equality through my partnership model and social influence for ourselves and our community members.

Sometimes these actions will not be rewarded. There is always risk of labeling and name calling by those who feel threatened or who are in fear of competition. Some will understand that there is room for this, and the outcome will be beneficial.

PROFESSIONAL

Using your femininity and charisma professionally can take many forms, from the simple to the complex. In this instance, it seems pertinent to use a case study where I had to step into a home-building project that had gone awry twice in the process from design, to approvals, to construction, and subcontractors. I use it because it was so emotional and challenging for the people involved and because the project went so smoothly once it was taken in hand. It was the use of charisma, as well as focused determination, flexibility, and respect that enabled it to be completed on time and on budget under adverse conditions. None of the men thought it could be done on time or on budget.

CASE STUDY
Design/Build Custom Home

A custom home is built, landscaped, and completed, from framing to finish, in 5.5 months.

After returning from a trip out of state, the husband arrived home, waving some architectural drawings in hand. He wanted to remodel the couple's custom home. The drawings were not in alignment with other houses in the neighborhood, and the neighbors took an immediate dislike for the proposed remodel. They went up in arms to the city planning department, and the contention began. The husband tried to negotiate a few times with the planning department, but ended up getting in a difficult situation with the city, as well. Things were not looking good from any perspective, and it appeared the process could be roadblocked.

Zoe took a look at the drawings and saw the process that needed to happen. She knew the following:

1. New plans would need to be drawn
2. This could take time and the process needed to be expedited/How?
3. Architectural input would be needed to navigate the planning department
4. Engineers and concrete would be needed, as well as a building crew
5. Framing, interior, exteriors
6. Appliance selection and orders
7. Moving the owners into short-term housing
8. Designers could be accessed through her network and her own skill-set
9. She would need buy-in and cooperation from people she could trust
10. The best way to get people you can trust is to create them by being one

She made some calls to a local CAD Master and had new plans drawn in detail, managing a whole new design process that was different, but aligned with a modernization of the old style neighborhood. She invited neighbors in to show them, from various points in the house, the views that were there were and painted a picture in their minds and in their experience of the views there would be. In so doing, she was able to get neighbors to rewrite their letters of opposition into letters of support.

Zoe went to planning meetings and negotiated with the six city planners in front of a room packed with folks from both sides of the disagreement. In the area, people have had their building projects held up for six months to three years. She negotiated through a system of agreements. The first meeting gave her the lay of the land in terms of hearing arguments, learning personalities, and any incestuous relationships. She acted on the redesign quickly, setting up to make the next meeting in two weeks. This was a systematic approach and demanded the approach of a mediator. She has assessed the planners and commission successfully, and at their refusal to pass the house, she set about a series of drills that successfully backed the planners into a corner through agreements. She did it so quickly they were caught off guard and actually said at the end, "We wish you had not done that." That solidified their unspoken commitment to honor their agreements.

Zoe and the CAD Master made the changes to the design, and in the planning meeting two weeks later, they were approved. So it began. The husband again took over the project, only to run into roadblocks again two months later with an inexperienced framing crew. Zoe was once again called in.

She made calls and pulled from resources to begin the build. She hired framers, who tented and put up the home quickly. Every sub was a referral, assessed and analyzed by Zoe based on the principles of honesty and open communication. The working agreements stood, and the house was up in 5.5 months. No one had seen it done before. She handled all the billing and was prompt and on the job daily. One behavior that was mentioned later was that she always went to each person on the site, no matter their role or position and spoke to them personally. She never missed one.

Other workers on the site were convinced her attitude and teammanship were what got the job done so quickly. Everyone was working together as one unit, even though they had never met in their lives. The common goal united them, and it was accomplished with the hardwood floor guy, tile guys, stucco finishers and kitchen cabinet guy all working at the same time, while the electrician finished, as well. On any traditional job site, many of these subs would never have met or known each other.

The Personal Approach of Charisma

One part of Zoe's approach was to work one-on-one with each person on the job—to discuss and flush out any personal issues or aspects that might conflict with their jobs or anything they might need to make their lives better, from referrals to counseling. Her mindset transferred to every man on the job, and they changed from the concept of "it can't be done" to "it will be done." And it was done with joy.

Each member of the team became a resource for the other. During the entire project, there was only one disagreement, and it lasted all of about 15 minutes before Zoe created a plastic wall to separate crew members and their work.

Team Training

This was a form of team training—as all of the sub would have been independent of each other, they learned interdependence. As an immediate result, the team members achieved better client awareness and better client relationships. These subs have gone on to manage client relationships more successfully than ever before, even without a general overseeing them. Not only have the team members become more solution oriented, they've become more business oriented as they now recognize business opportunities within existing clients and strategize how to make the most of them.

In conclusion, Zoe achieved:

- A mindset shift that demonstrated subs can work together at the same time with the right attitude in place being demonstrated by leaders.

- Greater business development awareness within all crew members, as well as better client relationship awareness and management.

- **A reduction of standard building costs from $4.0-5.0/sq ft. to $2.60/sq ft. for the entire project.**

SOCIAL

Your everyday life

Many people would probably not characterize themselves as FLIRTing on a daily basis, but when they think about it, they realize they have also been engaged in flirting. In my research, I spoke with men and women about the results and level of pleasure they experienced doing what might usually be mundane household chores. Here are some of the things people said:

"Dealing with a clerk at the DMV or somebody at Ross Dress-For-Less, or even at Wholefoods, has become a pleasurable

experience. When I'm engaging with the people who work in the places I do business, joking around with them, it seems to make them feel comfortable with me. I'm treating them with recognition and supporting them in feeling good, regardless of what they're doing," related one interviewee.

He talked at great length about how remarkable it is to feel engaged with others. It made the trips more fun, and the energy was dynamic. "What's remarkable to me is that we can walk in the door of the bank and everybody starts laughing, you know? They feel good about us being there."

"I know from talking to some of these people and by the way they react it's extremely rare during the course of their day. Not many people do this."

"Most people just go in there and get their form stamped, get their money from the bank, talk about the weather, you know, don't really talk to the cashier at the checkout line. They don't engage with them on a personal level. It's a non-emotional level that does not recognize the person helping you is in fact human."

"People gravitate to this type of engagement. When it comes to getting help at the bank, I am now on friendly terms with the people working there, and they are interested, simply based on feeling good to help solve problems that might come up. I have gotten extraordinary help as a result of developing relationships from checks being cashed or held to personal notification of balances, etc. They let me know they are going beyond their normal routine and are doing so because of our personal relationship. "

We've become very egocentric and narcissistic in our thinking; we really can't recognize anything outside of our immediate radius, whether that's six inches outside of our body or three feet, especially when we're walking in public areas. So many people walk around completely tensed up and angry, so in their head and negative thought process or memory, they forget to notice that it's an incredible day

FLIRTONOMICS

outside. Their body language and facial expression tells us this as we see them en route.

FLIRT is a way of getting outside your head and noticing there's other people around. When you engage positively with them, you've just left your old thoughts behind and shut the door for a minute. It's important and vital for your health and longevity. Interaction spurs compassion, empathy, and affection. Think about what a difference this could mean in society.

ROMANTIC

Romance is a dance. It is also a matter of understanding yourself and the person you are hoping to attract. There are three steps in romance.

1. Attract
2. Retain
3. Entertain

How to attract men in person or via online dating and maintain the attraction and attention seems to be something everyone wants to know. Flirting should be done every day with your mate. Men are attracted to beauty, but they are not captivated by it for more than a moment. They like mystery, allure, and humor. They like femininity and sex appeal, as well as nurture.

Which island are you?

Are you the island someone wants to live on, vacation on, or visit? Just think about this for a second. It will tell you a lot about your romantic relationships. Be honest. Of course, there is always variety in this, but in general you will fall primarily into one of these three categories. Naturally, you can assess which island the person you are interacting with is, as well.

Vacation Island: Are you the person people call when they want to have fun, a "friends with benefits" experience, or someone others don't consider to be relationship material? Are the people you meet constantly asking you out for drinks or to go away for the weekend, but not willing to make any more of a commitment? Perhaps you appear unstable to them or inconsistent. Sometimes it's a matter of you making them feel excited, but not safe. It's one thing to jump out of a plane with a novice and another to jump out with an expert. They see you as dependent playmate, not as a partner willing to do more than play.

Visiting Island: Are you the island they like to visit? Do you end up in situations where the people you meet only want to spend a brief amount of time with you and call infrequently? Are you someone people only like in small doses? Maybe you are a friend with benefits or too intense, sloppy, distracted, or appear disinterested yourself after a period of time. They may see you as a partner, but they see potential problems with the partnership in communication or other styles.

Living Island: This is the island they want to live on—it makes them feel safe, taken care of, and at home. Do you find yourself in a relationship with the person you just met over dinner? They feel relaxed around you, while they are also attracted at the same time. In fact, your cooking dinner or playing with your kids is exciting to them and makes them feel powerful. They are interested in taking care of you and working with you as a partner. They see you as partner, not dependent. It does not really matter which island other people are because you can only change yourself, and it is you doing the attracting. If you are the visiting island or vacation island, you might want to change some of your behaviors and attitudes if you are looking for a committed relationship.

Every island has its place; it's about realizing you may be acting as one type when you want to be treated like the other. If you are looking for a long-term romantic relationship and people are only looking to spend limited time with you, it is you who needs to change since you have no control over anyone but yourself. When we keep attracting the same types, it's time to look in the mirror.

FLIRTATION SKILLS

Learn the power of flirting in your romantic interests

Men are engaged more visually, while women are more engaged by what they hear. This makes what you wear and how you put yourself together for romance and your relationships important. Showing a little more skin or leg or flipping your hair is attractive to men. Flirting lets you show your brains and your beauty. You can flirt anywhere. It's so easy!

Learning to flirt is part of the act of engagement and learning to carry on a conversation that reflects the speed of your mind and your sense of humor, as well as your sex appeal. In online dating, the rapport is developed from afar. Your sense and pace of your words needs to be humorous with flirtatious calls to action. Men want intrigue and sex appeal; they can be one and the same. Flirting with men involves allure, mystery, intelligence, and class. You need some attitude and a sense of humor or excitement. Tell them what makes you excited-even if it is poetry-they want tips about you.

- Engage in a way that is fun, simple, and addresses them specifically.

- Do not waste people's time. Always be respectful and aware of their body language, which will tell you all you need to know about their comfort level with the conversation.

- Create sexual tension by alluding to sensual things or offering word-play that provides that visual for a man.

- Have fun. That is what flirting is all about.

- Think of something funny, a line from a movie, a song, a poem to engage with.

- Appeal to their interests to find common areas.

Be mysterious, alluring, and teasing by not giving them too much information. Understand and use sex-appeal when you meet and when you engage in emails without talking directly about sex. Do not text a lot. Do not tell everything to him; do not talk about your past relationships and never your sexual exploits. No matter what anyone says, men do not want to compete with a mystery man or woman (and neither do you).

Pay close attention to learning your counterpart's language and use mirroring to give them 110% of your attention. Having so much of your attention will be disconcerting and exciting. That is flirtatious, sexy, and fun.

CHAPTER 9

Conclusion

This is not really a conclusion as much as it is the beginning of a whole new way of looking at the world, considering what we each bring to the table, and serving it up in a delicious way that makes a positive impact. You are your own catalyst, and your personal assets are the tools you discover and learn to use with the precision of an expert. Your personal assets make up a diversified portfolio for life that shift and need re-balancing via asset allocation from time to time.

While some people may appear to have it easy because of their physical beauty, we now know that femininity can be "developed" and charisma can be learned. It is not only about doing a realistic assessment of your strengths, but also about overcoming your weaknesses. When people are physically and socially attractive, they can only leverage these two things as far as they act with intelligence and understanding of their intentions. Notwithstanding, physical and social skills do not override intention in human interactions. People who act in manipulation and use their extra traits to abuse others usually end of getting what they deserve in one form or another. People who inflict pain on others can never be truly happy nor have good people around them. This is why your intention is so important.

There is power in leveraging your personal capital from femininity, to charisma and vital energy. Your personal power comes in harnessing these assets and channeling them in the right directions where you can create the most impact, rather than letting them overflow irresponsibly. Yes, there is a certain responsibility that comes with honing your skills and you ability to influence others. If you are a black-belt in karate, then you are essentially a lethal weapon. The same can be said for people who have really honed their personal assets. Irresponsible acts include asking people to do or give up things you have no right to ask them to... or asking people for things you know they will have difficulty saying "No" to.

It is often hard to say no to a beautiful women or a charming man... they can sell you anything. The problem comes when they lack the ethics, values, or awareness to keep from asking unaccredited investors to invest (buy what they should not).

I researched ancient goddesses and mythology, reaching back into history to crystallize the concepts I use in my workshops. These are meant to give you some basis and grounding of the possibilities, as well as to help you recognize the essence that is already you. Durga and Ishtar, ancient Tibetan and Hindu goddesses, manifest the power of the feminine in all her forms. **She is not wearing a petticoat or holding a bag of Twinkies. She rides a lion and performs all the duties of the modern woman openly and in leadership. I'm borrowing her lion for you to climb on.**

I suggest the acknowledgement of what you know deep down to be true and use it as a pathway into your personal power as a woman. Understand your role is not one of the virgin martyr, but one of high leadership and access to all that makes you human, increasing your communication with the world at large. It is a dance and an encounter brought into modern day thought –at least that is my goal.

We call it FLIRTonomics because of the power of FLIRT or energetic engagement that lights the fire within others. It is not a waste or misleading when done with right intentions. We must tend to the flame and use it for its many purposes: to cause warmth, heat, light, purify, cook, and protect. It is a

CONCLUSION

win-win in the game of energy, health, and vitality and in making our jobs worth doing. Humor is essential for healthy humans.

Although FLIRTonomics is a book primarily for women, my work, like my flirting, has no gender, social, economic, or age bias. I work with individuals and groups as a project manager, coach, and catalyst to get things moving quickly. Some of this work involves personal brand development, which crystallizes the self-talk into a personal brand creation and delivery. My work with C-level executives and entrepreneurs helps them reframe their thinking about themselves and how they run their companies, allowing them to leverage their ROI from tens of thousands into millions of dollars. In the process, they find new ways of communicating with their wives, husbands, daughters, partners, sons, co-workers, and employees. My approach is holistic because it involves inspiration, behavioral, and intellectual change.

For more information on me, my workshops, or how to work with me, please visit www.zoesexton.com or www.flirtonomics.net. You may also contact me directly at zoe@zoesexton.com.

RESOURCES & RECOMMENDED READING

Lipstick & Politics: http://lipstickandpolitics.com/

Homer, Karen. *Things a Woman Should Know About Style.* London: Carlton Group, 2003. Print.

Salzberg, Sharon. *Loving Kindness: The Revolutionary Art of Happiness.* Boston & London: Shambhala, 2004. Print.

Hesselbein, Frances, Marshall Goldsmith, and Richard Beckhard, eds. *The Leader of The Future.* San Francisco, CA: Jossey-Bass, 1996. Print.

Wainwright, Gordon R. *Body Language.* Illinois, Chicago: NTC Group, 1993. Print.

Faulkner, Mary. *Women's Spirituality: Power and Grace.* Charlottesville, VA: Hampton Roads, 2011. Print.

Hakim, Catherine. *Erotic Capital.* New York, NY: Basic Books, 2011. Print.

Fieger, Hank. *Behavior Change: A View from the inside out.* New York: Morgan James, 2009. Print.

McTaggart, Lynne. *The Bond.* New York, NY: Free Press, 2011. Print.

Hansen, Mark Victor, and Robert G. Allen. *The One Minute Millionaire.* New York, NY: Harmony Books, 2002. Print.

Block, Peter. *Flawless Consulting*. San Francisco, CA: Jossey-Bass/Pfeiffer, 1981. Print.

Scumaci, Dondi. *Designed For Success*. Lake Mary, Florida: Excel Books, 2008. Print.

Levinson, Kate. *Emotional Currency*. Berkeley: Celestial Arts, 2011. Print.

Northrup, Christiane. *Women's Bodies, Women's Wisdom*. New York, NY: Bantam Books, 1998. Print.

CPSIA information can be obtained at www.ICGtesting.com
Printed in the USA
LVOW091730260712

291700LV00013B/41/P